ENJOY

John Markarian

MEN OF GRANITE

Andy Hagopian
AAHYI

by
Dan Manoyan

Dan Manoyan

authorHOUSE®

AuthorHouse™
1663 Liberty Drive, Suite 200
Bloomington, IN 47403
www.authorhouse.com
Phone: 1-800-839-8640

First published by AuthorHouse 10/15/2007

ISBN: 978-1-4343-4269-0 (sc)
ISBN: 978-1-4343-4268-3 (hc)

Printed in the United States of America
Bloomington, Indiana

This book is printed on acid-free paper.

Cover design by Melissia Ward.

DEDICATION

Men of Granite is dedicated to Ed and Elaine, who respectively taught me a love of sports and literature.

It is dedicated to Eddie and Randy, my own state champions.

And finally, it is dedicated to the forgotten 1.5 million Armenian martyrs, who died at the hands of the Ottoman Empire during World War I. Their souls will not rest until the descendants of the criminals acknowledge their slaughter for what it was...genocide.

TABLE OF CONTENTS

'Tis, finally, the Man, who, lifted high,
Conspicuous object in a Nation's eye,
Or left unthought of in obscurity,
Who, with a toward or untoward lot,
Prosperous or adverse, to his wish or not,
Plays, in the many games of life, that one
Where what he most doth value must be won.
Whom neither shape of danger can dismay,
Nor thought of tender happiness betray;
Who, not content that former worth stand fast,
Looks forward, persevering to the last,
From well to better, daily self-surpast:
Who, whether praise of him must walk the earth
For ever, and to noble deeds give birth,
Or he must fall to sleep without his fame,
And leave a dead unprofitable name,
Finds comfort in himself and in his cause;
And, while the mortal mist is gathering, draws
His breath in confidence of Heaven's applause:
This is the happy Warrior; this is he
Whom every man in arms should want to be.

> – excerpted from "The Character of the Happy
> Warrior," a poem by William Wordsworth
> (1770-1850).

1. THE HAPPY WARRIORS

Legend has it that the Warriors of Granite City became "The Happy Warriors" 12 years before that hardscrabble southwestern Illinois steel town on the Mississippi River, enjoyed its ultimate celebration.

The year was 1928 and the high school's football team had just finished a perfect season with a 9-0 record and championship of the prestigious Southwestern Illinois Conference. At the same time, Al Smith, the man who had been dubbed "The Happy Warrior," by Franklin D. Roosevelt in his nominating speech at the Democratic convention, was pervading the national consciousness in his bid to become president of the United States. The scholarly Roosevelt loved the William Wordsworth poem, said to be dedicated to the memory of Lord Nelson, and Roosevelt passed the moniker on to his political mentor.

An anonymous sports writer for the Granite City Press-Record, noting how the football Warriors, like Wordsworth's Happy Warrior, "played fair, absorbed victory without boast, fights to the end and makes victory his habit," drew a parallel. The Warriors became "The Happy Warriors" in print that fall and the name stayed with them and future Granite City teams for years to come.

Smith lost to Herbert Hoover in his bid to become president and The Great Depression swept the nation. Times were hard everywhere in America and Granite City was no exception. But the Warriors never lost their fighting spirit.

By 1940, the nation was pulling out of its economic doldrums, but there was another cloud on the horizon. For the second time in 25 years, the dogs of war were barking in Europe, signaling the coming of the most devastating conflict this planet would ever know.

At the same time, there were changes sweeping Granite City as well. For years, Granite City had been a city divided by a set of railroad tracks, a man-made barrier that pared the city into two separate but unequal sections. On the east side of the tracks was the city's downtown and the residences of the long-established settlers of city. Some would call those people, the "Haves" of Granite City.

To the west of the tracks were the bustling steel mills and the humble homes of the immigrant laborers who made the factories hum. Those relative newcomers to this country and their families – Hungarians, Macedonians, Armenians, Yugoslavs and Mexicans mainly – were the "Have-nots" of Granite City.

The discrimination those immigrants faced was more of a subtle nature than the overt racism that faced African-Americans in those days. While it wasn't a tangible discrimination, it was the proverbial elephant in the parlor. It was something that undeniably existed and residents of both sides of the track knew it existed. It was something that Smith, as an Irish-American immigrant and the first Catholic to run for the presidency of the United States, knew all too well.

It was a discrimination of attitudes and perceptions, but nonetheless it was discrimination. It manifested itself in ways such as staying away from "those people" or not wanting "one of them" to date your daughter. It even was a factor in how Granite City High School's athletics teams were chosen.

As we have seen in the years since, athletics can be a great equalizer and agent for change in this country. A high school basketball team, the 1940 Granite City Happy Warriors, changed that city – more specifically that city's perception of its immigrant population – forever.

Not every Granite City team since 1928 had been a happy team. There were as many downs as ups in this city that nightly watches the sun set over the Mississippi River in the direction of St. Louis. There was hurt and there were hard feelings.

For years, the immigrant talent, especially in basketball, was left unharvested. It took a player of the magnitude of Andy Phillip, a member of the Naismith Basketball Hall of Fame and the product of Hungarian immigrants, to open the doors for the others.

Phillip came onto the Granite City basketball scene in 1938 as a sophomore. By 1940, seven of the 10 players on the Granite City squad were of immigrant stock, including all five starters.

This was a team that would take Granite City beyond "happy." It brought a sense of pride to the city and all its inhabitants that had never been there before.

The players of this squad were happy long before they became Warriors. Most of all, they were happy about being citizens of the United States. Their parents' horror stories of tyranny, hardship and genocide in the worlds that they had left behind were well known to these teenage boys.

After what their parents had lived through, it's reasonable to conclude these Warriors were just happy to be living. Period.

Four of the Happy Warriors – Andy "Huggy" Hagopian, Evon Parsaghian, Sam Mouradian and John Markarian – were of Armenian extraction. Their parents were among the fortunate few survivors of the of Ottoman Turks' genocide of its Armenian subjects during World War I. That holocaust, which emboldened Adolph Hitler to mastermind the annihilation of the Jews in World War II, witnessed as many as 1.5 million Armenian deaths.

Philip, who was born Andras Fulop, was the undisputed star and captain of the Granite City basketball team. He was of Magyar extraction from the plains of Hungary. Danny Eftimoff's family came to this country from Macedonia.

George Gages' people came from Yugoslavia. The seven sons of immigrants teamed up with three local boys – Ed (Ebbie) Mueller and Ed Hoff, both of German extraction, and Everett Daniels, whose lineage was Scotch and Irish – to form one of the most intriguing teams in Illinois' schoolboy history.

Outside of Phillip, who went on to stardom at the University of Illinois and in the NBA, and the freakishly-athletic Parsaghian, it wasn't a team bestowed with extreme gifts of athleticism. But, perhaps because of where its team members had come from, it was a team that played its best basketball when its collective backs were to the wall and facing defeat.

At the 16-team state finals on the campus of the University of Illinois, in Champaign, Granite City easily won its first game. But the Happy Warriors' true mettle came through when the tournament field was pared to eight.

Granite City trailed its opponents after three quarters in its last three games of the state tournament. In its quarterfinal game against Dundee, Granite City trailed, 28-26, but won 35-30. In the semifinals, the Warriors trailed Moline, 29-26, but rallied to win 41-38.

In the championship game against Herrin, playing without its sparkplug guard Hagopian, who had suffered a shoulder injury against Moline earlier that afternoon, Granite City trailed, 16-15, but eked out a 24-22 victory on Parsaghian's dramatic last-second layup.

But the Warriors had made their biggest comeback two weeks before the state finals, held at the University of Illinois' Huff gym in Champaign. Thanks to a quirky proviso of the Illinois High

School Association at that time, runners-up in the state's regional tournaments – the first stage of the tournament – advanced to the next stage, the sectionals, along with the regional champions.

Granite City lost to its archrival, Wood River in the regional championship game, but because of the rule that was in place, advanced to the sectional. Given a second chance, the Warriors ousted Wood River the next time around – the fourth time the two teams had played that season – 36-32, in the sectional championship game.

It was the first time in Illinois high school basketball history that a state champion had lost a tournament game en route to its championship.

"No one has ever called Granite City the greatest of Illinois state high school champions," wrote Champaign News-Gazette sports editor and long-time state tournament observer Jack Prowell, in an article that appeared in the 1952 Illinois State Tournament official program.

"But it surely holds the honor of being the greatest when the chips were down. The pressure was never too great for those sons of Lincoln Place, a foreign settlement in Granite City.

"Perhaps their very background, filled with stories of ancestral battles for life in their homelands before migrating to America had something to do with it."

Indeed it did. Basketball, even at the state championship level, was child's play compared to the life and death battles fought by their parents. It was a single-minded team of aptly-named Warriors, conceived in the mountains of Turkey and the plains of Europe, and forged in the teeming steel mills of Granite City.

"I guess we hated to lose," Hagopian would say in later years. "I'm sure it had a lot to do with where we came from."

2. EXIT FROM HELL

By his own admission, John Markarian didn't play much of a role in Granite City's exploits at the state finals in Champaign. He was only added to the team roster for the state tournament when another bench player, Earl Kunneman, suffered from appendicitis late in the season.

Markarian, a modest man, to this day feels awkward talking about that most glorious season in Granite City history because of the small role he played. Yet Markarian cherishes his one moment in the spotlight.

In the closing seconds of the state championship game, with Granite City clinging to a precarious two-point lead over Herrin. Warriors coach Byron Bozarth sent the seldom-used Markarian into the game with instructions to inbounds the basketball to Andy Phillip and tell Phillip to heave the basketball as high as he could into the Huff Gym rafters, as the game's final seconds ticked away.

A violation on the inbounds play, foiled Bozarth's strategy and gave Herrin one last desperate shot at tying the game, but the thought was there. While Markarian, who was a junior classman at the time of the state championship, didn't play a major role in the team's ultimate success, how he came to be a member of that team is a miracle in itself. His story, and ultimately the story of the Happy Warriors, began half a world away in the Eastern Turkey village of Erzurum at the outbreak of World War I.

Kaspar Kakligian, who later changed his surname to Markarian, was living a peaceful life there with his wife Juhar and his two daughters. But life for Turkey's Christian Armenian minority would take a tragic turn for the worse in November of 1914, when the Ottoman Empire, led by the Young Turks, entered World War I on the side of the Germans.

The Turks, hoping to expand their Middle Eastern empire into the Caucasus region and regain lost territories in the Balkans, were naturally suspicious of the Armenians, who had coexisted for centuries on their native lands as loyal, albeit second-class citizens, of Turkey. Early in the war, the Turks suffered a setback on the eastern front at the hands of the Russians at Sarikamish and it was discovered that some soldiers of Armenian descent were among the Russian troops.

For the Turks, that was justification enough for what was to follow, the systemic annihilation of 1.5 million of its Armenian citizens. As a first step, all Armenian men enlisted in the Turkish army were disarmed and executed by February of 1915.

Next, the Turks targeted the Armenian intellectuals and leaders. On April 24, 1915, the Ottomans rounded up and executed 250 Armenian intellectuals and cultural leaders. April 24 is marked to this day by Armenians around the world as "Holy Martyrs Day."

But what the Turks did next was the act that shocked the world and qualified their actions as a full-scale genocide. The Young Turks, under orders from Talaat Pasha, the regime's Minister of the Interior, ordered the systematic deportation of all its Armenians citizens.

The plan was to march the Armenians, most of who lived in their historic homeland of Eastern Turkey, south through the Deir el-Zor desert, with Syria as their ultimate destination. Most of them never made it.

Unspeakable atrocities awaited the Armenians at every step of their perilous journey. Gendarmes, commissioned by the Turks, as well as nomadic Kurds, were green lighted to plunder the never-ending caravans of defenseless women, children and elderly.

Markarian's mother Juhar and his two older sisters were among those making the perilous journey from Erzurum, which was just 100 miles from the Russian border and ground zero for the deportations. Kaspar headed east and joined the forming regiment of Armenian freedom fighters under the leadership of national hero General Antranig.

Kaspar returned to Erzurum after the war to search for his family, only to be told that they had all perished. The news was only half true, however.

Markarian's sisters, whose names, to this day are not known to him, both perished in the desert march. But Juhar miraculously survived to reach freedom, eventually crossing the Turkish border into Halab, which is now known as Aleppo, Syria.

"My sisters died of starvation," Markarian emotionally retold the story. "My mother didn't like to talk about what happened, but she said it was horrible. She said it was so bad that she saw parents drown their own children in the river to keep them from dying of starvation."

Although he is not sure, Markarian doesn't think his mother was hinting that she took matters into her own hands and ended her daughters' suffering.

"From what I can tell, it was mostly young boys who for some reason were killed by their own mothers," John said.

Kaspar, thinking his entire family had perished in the genocide, married another Armenian woman. The newlyweds headed east across Asia with the United States as their ultimate destination.

A daughter was born to the couple in Vladivostok, Siberia in 1919. The new family emigrated to the West Coast of the United States where Kaspar found work in the hops fields of Oregon and changed his name to Markarian.

Granite City already had a burgeoning population of Armenians, among other nationalities, and its steel mills were hiring. Kaspar had two older brothers living in Granite City so he knew there was opportunity for work in the mills, and he headed east.

But when he got to Granite City, Kaspar received some shocking news. He learned through a relative that Juhar was still alive. She had somehow managed to post the news in an Armenian language newspaper that circulated in the United States and the news was relayed to Kaspar.

Upon hearing the news, Kaspar's second wife left Granite City and headed east for New York on her own. She left behind her baby girl Arshalous (Arshig).

Soon thereafter, Juhar made her way to Granite City, where in 1922 she gave birth to a baby boy named Zohrab, later to be known as John Markarian.

"It's quite a story and I don't know all the details of course," Markarian said. "My father's second wife just left when she heard the news (of Juhar's survival).

"I don't know if they ever went through the paperwork (of a divorce) or what happened. But she left her child and that was my sister.

"It was our family."

Markarian's parents told their two surviving children as little as possible about their tragic past, but Juhar brought with her two markings that to this day are indelibly etched in John's mind.

"My mother had a scar over her eyebrow where she said a German soldier hit her with the butt of his rifle," John said. "And, she also had a tattoo on her wrist.

"It was an image of Jesus Christ. She said she would look at the image every day and pray. She said it was what helped her survive her ordeal."

3. THE FIRST TEMPEST-TOSSED ARRIVE

The city of Van is the furthest most major city of eastern Turkey, just 50 miles from the Iranian border and just 100 miles from what is today the border of the Republic of Armenia. In 1894, there was no Republic of Armenia, but Turkey shared a common border with its mortal enemy, the Russians.

Because of its strategic location, Van was a focal point for the first round of Armenian massacres by the Turks in the mid-1890's. Armenians, protesting the Ottoman Empire's policy of second-class citizenship for its minority Christian population (excessive taxes and limited property rights), incurred the ire of the Sultan Abdul Hamid II, who ruled the Empire from 1876 to 1908. It is estimated that Hamid, who was dubbed "The Great Assassin" by British Prime Minister Gladstone, was responsible for the deaths of over 200,000 Armenians between 1894 and 1896.

Van, a city with one of the largest Armenian populations in the Empire, particularly felt the wrath of Hamid. According to Peter Balakian's book, "The Burning Tigris" to protect their homes from looting, a group of Armenians, estimated between 600 and 700, took up arms against the Turks in the Aikesdan section of Van in June of 1896.

Abdul Hamid's response was to send in four battalions of infantry and cavalry to put down the insurrection. The fight raged from June 3 through June 11 with the Turks unable to disarm the Armenians.

Hamid eventually sued for peace, assuring France and England that he would guarantee "the lives and safety" of the Armenians of Van if the super powers would help broker the peace. The Armenian fighters, who made it clear they were only acting in self-defense, agreed to leave the country via Iran, which shares a border with Turkey.

Nearly 1,000 of them laid down their arms and agreed to be escorted out of the country by Turkish troops. They never made it to Iran. Along the way they were murdered by Turkish troops and Kurdish pillagers.

Sooran "Sam" Hagopian was born in 1895, a year before the first insurrection of Van occurred. Needless to say the climate in which he was raised in Van was such that many Armenians took the first opportunity available to leave their homeland and seek safe haven.

By 1913, Sooran was an 18-year-old man and in the relatively calm days before the Great War would again rock the worlds of Turkish Armenians, he chose to leave the country. He emigrated from Turkey to the United States and heeding the advice of Armenians already here, headed straight for Granite City.

"The Armenians wrote to one another and told each other about Granite City," said Andy Hagopian, explaining his father's thinking. "If there was one Armenian here, pretty soon there would be 100. They congregated here.

"When they first came here it wasn't to stay. They all wanted to make just enough money to go back home."

Unfortunately, the events of World War I, of which the Ottoman Empire's genocide of 1.5 Armenians was a disastrous outgrowth, precluded the Armenians of Granite City from returning to their homeland. There was no homeland after that.

There was an Armenian nation set aside by the powers that be in the Treaty of Sevres. But soon that tiny nation was gobbled up by the emergent Soviet Union. After leaving one tyrannical nation, the thought of returning to another wasn't an option that most Armenian-Americans took seriously.

Relocating to Soviet Armenia wasn't an option for Sooran, but claiming an Armenian bride was a high priority. In 1920, with the war over, he took leave of his job at a Granite City steel mill and headed for Istanbul in search of an Armenian wife.

There, he met another Armenian from Van, who had survived the genocide by escaping to Yerevan, behind Russian lines. The man introduced Sooran to his sister, Nevart. Sooran and Nevart (Rose) were married and returned to Granite City where they would raise a family of one boy, Antranig (Andy), and three girls, Alees (Alice), Seta (Sadie) and Vanoohi (Mary).

"My father went back to his job at the steel mills and soon I was born," said Andy, who was named after the great Armenian freedom fighter of World War I, General Antranig. "I've been here ever since.

"My parents never talked much about what happened in the old country and we didn't pursue it. It wasn't such a big conversation piece as it is today. Everybody was just concentrating on making a living and raising their families."

The parents of Sam Mouradian and Evon (Yervant) Parsaghian were both from the same hometown in Turkey, the town of Moush, located on the north end of the Plain of Sasun, the historic homeland of ancient Armenia. Again, it was the scene of bloody insurrection and retaliation by the Turks in the 1890s. Avedis Parsaghian left there in 1911, and according to a 1940 story by Pat Harmon in the Champaign (Ill.) News-Gazette, "rolled up all his possessions in a large handkerchief and pulled out" of the town. According to the story, Parsaghian had saved enough money by 1920 to "send" for his wife Ankin.

Harmon's story claimed that Asadoor Mouradian, also originally from Moush, did much the same as Parsaghian. He apparently emigrated from Moush to Granite City in 1913 and somehow tracked down his wife in Smyrna after the war.

The other immigrant parents of the 1940 Granite City team, the parents Andy Phillip, George Gages and Dan Eftimoff, didn't leave their homelands at the point of bayonets, yet still had compelling reasons to come to the United States and ultimately to Granite

City. Like every other immigrant who has washed up to the docks at Ellis Island, they wanted a better life for themselves and their families.

John Fulop, who anglicized his name to Phillip like so many immigrants arriving at Ellis Island, was of Magyar lineage. According to the Harmon story, both of the Phillip parents were from the state of Havash in Hungary.

John Fulop had been an officer in a Hungarian Calvary unit, stationed in Budapest, around the turn of the century before coming to the United States. The Hungarians were among the first wave of immigrants to reach Granite City in the 1890s and Fulop found his way there after a brief stint in Dearborn, Mich., in the early 1900s.

Like the Armenians, Fulop returned to the old country to find a bride. Around 1916, he returned to Hungary and found his 15-year-old bride.

Eftimoff's father George immigrated to the United States in 1905 at the age of 15. He was a Macedonian from Bulgaria.

Little is known about Gages' father, who came to this country from Yugoslavia. The elder Gages died in 1939, but not before producing three sons and three daughters with Susie Gages, a native of Padina, Yugoslavia.

4. FORGING A CITY

Like all of the other Midwestern steel towns that rose in the latter days of America's Industrialization, Granite City is not a garden spot. Functional certainly, with its access to the Mississippi River to the west and its 35-mile link of the Terre Haute and Alton Railroad that divided the town and its people, but never pretty.

While the railroad was a lifeline to the steel industry of Granite City, it was a line of demarcation to the town's residents. "The wrong side of the tracks" wasn't a song title or a laughing matter to the mostly immigrant residents of Lincoln Place, "Hungary Hollow" and West Granite. It was a way of life.

Directly to the east of the tracks was the once bustling Granite City downtown that had everything a town of that size (22,974 residents in 1940) would have. There were hotels (The Molthrop, the Hommert, the Lauff), dry goods and clothing stores, bakeries and food stores, restaurants, Sperry's Confectionary and Uzell's Drugstore and Ice Cream Parlor. There also were several banks and the Washington Movie Theater. Other focal points of the downtown were City Hall, a YMCA and the Granite City Library.

Further to the east was Granite City Community High School, which moved to its current site on Madison Avenue in 1921. East of the tracks is where the elite of Granite City did business and where they lived.

If east of the tracks was functional, no frills and modest, west of the tracks, by comparison, was bleak. Not that it was different than other immigrant communities of the time, but the houses were for the most part tiny two-bedroom bungalows that sometimes housed families of eight or more. It had its businesses, taverns, barber shops, food stores and coffee shops, but for the most part its residents had to walk downtown for most of their needs.

The most prominent buildings of the area west of the tracks were Granite City's gigantic steel mills. Steel came to Granite City gradually and almost by accident.

Young German immigrants, Frederick G. and William F. Niedringhaus, fresh from Westphalia, Germany, were instrumental in charting Granite City's future away from agriculture and toward industry. They arrived in St. Louis in the 1850's as tinners, and by 1866 had formed their own business – St. Louis Stamping Works – which stamped out tin kitchen utensils.

In a trip to his native Germany in 1865, William was introduced to a new process of making utensils, where a white glossy coating was added to the tin. The product was known as graniteware because ground granite was used as the basic coating material. The industry boomed and in 1892, the Niedringhauses, seeking to expand their production, purchased 3,500 acres of land across the river from St. Louis in an area that was then known as Kinderhook.

The city was incorporated in March of 1896 under the name of Granite City, named for Niedringhauses' growing in popularity Graniteware, the primary product of the St. Louis Stamping Company. Family members apparently lobbied the brothers to name the city "Niedringhaus," but William and Frederick decided Granite City would be a more appropriate name for their new city.

The company would change its name to NESCO (National Enameling and Stamping Company) in 1896 and the dye would be cast for unbridled growth in Granite City. Sheets of steel were needed as raw material for tea pots and other household utensils that NESCO was now cranking out. By the turn of the century, Granite City was home to four major steel mills – Granite City Steel Co., American Steel, Commonwealth Steel, and General Steel Casting.

While NESCO was the primary reason the steel mills initially moved to Granite City, the later mills produced steel for a variety of growing American industries. American Steel grew into the nation's largest producer of cast steel railroad freight car side frames, bolsters and couplers. Commonwealth also specialized in steel castings and railroad locomotives.

Andy Phillip's father, John, would rise at 3 a.m. every morning to walk to Commonwealth to fulfill his role as foreman. His basic job was to record the amount of work produced by each man under his direction and the workers were paid accordingly.

General Steel Casting, which employed most of Granite City's Armenian immigrant population, purchased Commonwealth in 1929 and continued its line of production. During World War II, the plant was converted into making anchors, armor hulls for tanks and navy guns castings. The plant was eventually closed in 1970.

Although working in mills was almost gulag-like, there was no shortage of takers for jobs. Of course concepts such as overtime, vacations and job security were distant dreams to the mill workers of Granite City in the early years of the 20th Century. Pay was subsistence level and it was based on how much a man was willing and able to do. Compensation in those days was based on the "piece work" system – workers were paid according to the number of pieces of work he was able to produce.

As the steel mills went up, so did Granite City's booming population. When the city was incorporated in 1896, it had a population of 992, but by 1920 there were 14,757 residents in Granite City.

By 1930 the city's population numbered 25,130 and it continued to grow until it reached a peak of 40,440 in 1970.

5. THE CHARACTER OF THE CITY

By the 1930s, Granite City was being called the "Pittsburgh of the West." The town's slogan was "We are the Industrial magnet of the West."

The city was literally bursting at the seams with the influx of Eastern Europeans, blacks and rural southerners into the area. Partly by design of the city fathers, all too happy to enforce the segregation practices that were still rampant in Southern Illinois at the time, and partly because of a desire of the groups to be among their own kind, the newcomers to Granite City lived in their own distinct areas.

The Hungarians, of which Phillip descended from, were the first of the Eastern European immigrants, arriving in Granite in large numbers in the late 1890s. They settled in the Lincoln Place neighborhood and most of them worked at NESCO. The area was originally known as "Hungary Hollow," but when times got rough during the depression of 1907, it was bastardized to "Hungry Hollow," a reflection of the hard times.

Next came waves of Bulgarians, Macedonians, Armenians, Yugoslavs and Mexicans. Like the Hungarians, the newcomers settled in the Lincoln Place neighborhood.

According to Andy Hagopian, the Armenian immigrants to the area saw Lincoln Place and Granite City as a temporary stopover.

"It was the same with all of them," he said. "All our parents came here with the same idea. They were going to make enough money and go back to the old country.

"But after what happened (in Turkey), there was no place for them to go back to. There was nothing left."

Perhaps surprisingly, despite the diversity of cultures and backgrounds, all the ethnics of Lincoln Place got along well for the most part.

"We were all in the same boat," Hagopian said of his formative years in Lincoln Place. "All of our folks worked in the mills and to the people downtown we were all 'Hunkies.'

"There were the "haves" and the "have-nots" and we were looked down on, there is no question. We were literally from the wrong side of the tracks."

While there was general harmony among the various ethnic groups that inhabited Lincoln Place, it could be a rough and tumble area. Because of a severe housing shortage in the area, single men tended to live in saloon/boarding houses, where drinking was sometimes the only cure for loneliness. The Yellow Dog, the Blue Goose, the Black Bear and the Big Four were among the most popular of those sorts of establishments.

While the immigrants may have been looked down upon by the Granite City elites, they were not the bottom of the barrel...in fact they were far from it. It could be argued that the southern whites, including a large group of immigrants from Dover, Tenn., were a notch below.

These rural, mostly uneducated whites dubbed "Hoosiers," settled in the West Granite neighborhood and, like the immigrants, tended to stay among their own kind. The only places their paths crossed with the foreigners were in the mills and Washington School, where all the kids from the wrong side of the tracks attended.

"They were in the same boat as we were. I'm sure the people downtown looked down their noses at the Hoosiers, too," Markarian recollected. "We all went to the same school and on the last day of school, we would always meet in a big field for a war.

"It was the Hunkies against the Hoosiers. We'd throw rocks, shoot BB guns at each other, you name it."

But there is no debate as to which group was at the absolute bottom of the socio-economic barrel of pre-World War II Granite City. While there was a sizable population of African-Americans working at the Granite City mills, they were not even allowed to live within the city limits.

They had their communities and schools – Venice and Madison – which were located just to the south of Granite City. Up until World War II, African

27

Americans only were welcome in Granite City as labor. As in so many communities in the South and lower Midwest at the time, there were unwritten laws that African-Americans were all too familiar with. In Granite City, African-Americans who lingered after 9 p.m., subjected themselves to harassment and sometimes much worse.

Dick King, who was the Granite City High School student body president in 1939 and later went on to become an actor on Broadway, has a unique perspective of his home town.

"Granite City was a very prejudiced city when I was a kid," King said. "One of the steel mills would blow a whistle at 9 o'clock and all the black people had to be out of town.

"The only black person who was allowed to stay in town was a shoe shine boy by the name of Johnny. He worked in front of the barbershop downtown on Washington Street and he slept in the basement at night."

"I think the discrimination started to break down after 1940," Hagopian said.

For the African-Americans who worked in Granite City, breaking down the barriers of racism had everything to do with the onset of World War II. For the immigrant stock of Granite City, it had more to do with winning a basketball championship.

6. LINCOLN PLACE CENTER

The immigrants who found their way to Granite City were there for one reason...to make a better life for themselves and their families. But as was the case wherever large pockets of immigrants were found in those days, there was a concern by the local citizenry that the newcomers posed a potential threat to the American way of life when they clustered in such large numbers.

To that end, executives of Granite City's Commonwealth Steel, in order to "Americanize" the immigrant families, proposed the building of a community center, or "settlement house" as such places were called in those days. Commonwealth would donate the materials, the red bricks, the mortar and, of course, the steel girders to build a center for the people of Lincoln Place, if the local citizenry would provide the labor.

"The Clubhouse," as it would be affectionately known by the generations of mostly young immigrants, would feature a gymnasium/auditorium, classrooms, an office and an outdoor playground. It was constructed and opened in 1921. Classes were offered in Americanization, citizenship, hygiene and English.

For the boys, there was woodworking and Boy Scouts. For the girls, there was sewing and Girl Scouts. Sunday school classes and kindergarten were also offered.

Brick by brick, the building took form – almost a cross between an Eastern Orthodox Church and a warehouse – at 822 Niedringhaus Ave., between Maple and Spruce Streets. All that was needed was the human touch, and that task fell to mighty mite Sophia Prather.

Prather, born in 1869 in Carlyle, Ill. could trace her American lineage back to the Revolutionary War. She was 52 years old when she left teaching to become the director of Lincoln Place Community House in 1921. For years she had taught at nearby Washington School, the elementary school of Lincoln Place and West Granite, but she considered her work at Lincoln Place a higher calling.

Miss Prather, a tiny woman who wore glasses, became known as "The little mother of Lincoln Place." And, like any good mother, she dispensed love and discipline in equal doses. Any rowdy who dared get out of line at Lincoln Place, soon found out who was the boss.

"Let's put it this way," Hagopian recalled. "Everyone knew who the boss was at Lincoln Place. Miss Prather would let you know in a hurry."

A letter to the editor of the Granite City Press-Record from an E. Naumoff, following Granite City's

1940 State Tournament run, illustrated how tough Miss Prather could be.

"Many a time she would switch the naked bodies of her boys when they did not respond to her knocks on the shower room door, which meant to the bathers that their allotted time under the showers was up. A few whacks always brought forth a feeling of respect for Miss Prather and obedience to rules naturally followed."

"Her children, at first meeting, either liked her or hated her, but during puberty and adolescence they liked and respected her without reservation."

The boys weren't the only ones who loved and respected Miss Prather.

"I remember she would eat at a little restaurant nearby and we would wait for her to open up the clubhouse," recalled Queenie Elieff, the sister of Dan Eftimoff. "I remember getting so excited when we would see her walking down the street to let us in.

"We all loved her, she would do anything for us, but she could be very tough, too. Once she caught me chewing gum and wouldn't allow me into the building for a week. I remember how envious I was of the other kids, watching them go inside."

While she could be a stern taskmaster, Miss Prather was also known for her heart of gold. The first rule of the Lincoln Place Center was "No gym shoes, no basketball." For many of the immigrant children, shoes were considered almost a luxury item and gym shoes were superfluous in their hard-working parents' eyes.

Miss Prather always rode to the rescue, however. For those too poor to afford gym shoes, she assigned odd jobs, sweeping the floor, dusting, tidying up the place.

Andy Phillip was among those too poor to own his own gym shoes so Miss Prather provided him with a pair. They were an unmatched set of sneakers, but to Phillip, they were golden shoes with wings.

"Miss Prather gave Andy those shoes to play basketball and he never forgot it," said his widow, Corky Phillip. "They weren't matched shoes, but he didn't care...they allowed him to get on the basketball floor and play basketball."

"I played in my stocking feet a lot of times," Hagopian said. "Who could afford shoes?"

Miss Prather devised a point system and when a child earned enough points, she would provide that child with gym shoes. No boy who desired to play basketball at Lincoln Place was left behind. Although she wasn't a basketball coach per se, Miss Prather was fond of the sport and saw it as a great tool for allowing the sometimes rambunctious children to blow off steam.

"(Prather) delegated floor time to the children who wanted to play," Hagopian said. "If you misbehaved, you didn't get to play.

"We ran to the clubhouse to play ball together every day. We just played and played and played. We were just having fun, initially. Outside of Andy Phillip, nobody was that outstanding."

Lincoln Place's basketball court was by no measurement "regulation." It was shorter than a regulation court and the steel girders that held up the roof, while providing creative fodder for trick shot artists, were a bane to the local two-handed set shooters who had an appreciable arc to their shot.

"We used to love to try to shoot it through the girders and make a basket," Markarian said. "Only fooling around though... You didn't mess around like that in a game."

Indeed, basketball was serious business at Lincoln Place. Win, and you stayed on the floor to play another game. Lose, and you sat and watched. While basketball was as foreign to the boys of Lincoln Place as the All-American sports of baseball and football, they were quick learners.

There was no formal coaching or teaching of the game at Lincoln Place. The older boys learned by playing and younger boys learned by watching the older boys.

So, they dribbled until they could skillfully navigate through a defense. They honed their two-handed set shots and their underhanded free throws until they could convert their shots with amazing proficiency. But mostly, they played games.

"It was all we had," Hagopian would say. "If we didn't have that gym, what would we do? What else did we have? We didn't have money to join the YMCA. Basketball was a big part of our lives."

There were no cliques at Lincoln Place. It wasn't the Bulgarians against the Yugoslavians or the Armenians against the Hungarians. Teams were chosen according to ability and the best teams ruled the floor.

"You were lucky to get court time because there were so many good players down there," Hagopian said. "But they chose up teams strictly on ability."

While competition was hot and heavy to get onto the floor, fighting was rare at Lincoln Place and certainly not tolerated by Miss Prather.

"It could be pretty rough," Hagopian said. "Sometimes, if you wanted to play, you had to muscle some of the older kids aside. But there was no fighting. We were all in the same boat."

Little did they know it at the time, but that "boat" would someday float Granite City to the Nirvana of Illinois schoolboy basketball. Seven members of the 1940 state championship team – Phillip, Hagopian, Parsaghian, Eftimoff, Gages, Markarian and Mouradian – would come from Lincoln Place Center.

It was estimated at the time that approximately 10 percent of Granite City High School's enrollment of 1,600 students came from the Lincoln Place neighborhood. Yet, seven of 10 team members including all five starters of the 1940 team were from that tiny slice of Granite City.

In 1939, the Granite City Park District took over operations of the Lincoln Park Center. To this day, the building is run by the Park District and serves the Lincoln Center Community.

Miss Prather passed away in 1937, three years before her greatest success story came to fruition. An elementary school in Granite City still bears her name, but her memory and the good work she did at Lincoln Place was remembered in 1940.

"Had her boys of Lincoln Place never won a state basketball title, they never would have forgotten Sophia Prather," said an article that appeared in the Granite City Press-Record under the headline of "Boys from 'Across the Tracks' Won Title for Sophia Prather," shortly after the team won the state championship.

"However, this triumph was a grand gesture to a woman who is dear to them all."

7. THE ARCHITECT

By all accounts, Byron Bozarth, the man who coached Granite City to the 1940 Illinois schoolboy championship was a soft-spoken, modest and dedicated man. He was described as "erudite and scholarly." He was a renaissance man, able to quote his literary hero, poet Walt Whitman, as readily as quote his athletic role model, legendary University of Illinois football coach Bob Zuppke.

In Granite City in the 1930's, Bozarth and the title "Coach" were as one. He WAS the athletic program in town. Literally a man for all seasons, both on off the playing fields, Bozarth coached football, probably his first love, in the fall. In the spring, he coached track.

Basketball, the sport in which he enjoyed his greatest success as a coach, was a tool for conditioning his track team when it was too cold to train outdoors.

Bozarth, a native of Staunton, Ill., was a three-sport athlete in his home town. From there he matriculated to the University of Illinois, where he didn't play any sports himself but became a disciple of Zuppke, whose all-encompassing coaching philosophy vaulted Illinois' football program into the national spotlight and became a road map for aspiring young coaches.

Bozarth, who affectionately came to be known as "Bozzi" in his adopted home town, began his coaching and teaching careers in his home town Staunton High School and then at Bunker Hill High School before coming to bustling Granite City in 1927.

Bozarth soon built a reputation for winning teams and fair play on the field, but if he had a shortcoming as a coach, it was that his vision for Granite City athletics didn't always stretch beyond the railroad tracks that separated that city. Whether it was a deliberate act of omission or an unconscious bias, Bozarth's early basketball teams did not take advantage of the ethnic talent that was being churned out at the Lincoln Place gym. A photo of his 1933 team shows not one ethnic player on board.

"There were plenty of good players before us, believe me," said Hagopian of his Lincoln Place predecessors. "I had a neighbor who had a backboard in his driveway and could shoot like nobody, but they wouldn't take him. The kids from Lincoln Place couldn't make his teams. That was the perception in the neighborhood at least.

"Bozarth was a good man, but he was also a politician, too. He had to deal with the businessmen and so forth who supported the team.

"We didn't have any clout in Lincoln Place. There were no school board members from there and the people down there didn't go to the games. They couldn't afford to pay to get in. Bozarth was under a lot of pressure from the community to play the kids from the right side of town."

Not everyone in Granite City would agree with Hagopian's assertion that Bozarth had a prejudice against players from Lincoln Place.

"I would disagree with that," said Kenny Parker, who was one of the stars of the 1938 team and later went on to play with Phillip at Illinois. "Andy (Phillip) and Evon (Parsaghian) were on that 1938 team that went to the state tournament.

"But I don't think (Bozarth) cared where the players came from. He wanted to put the best team on the floor."

Several events transpired that eventually convinced Bozarth that using the talent from west of the tracks for his basketball team might be the way to go. First, there was the fiasco of the 1938 Granite City team that had qualified for that year's "Sweet 16" of the state tournament. It was, to that point, the most successful team that Bozarth had ever coached.

In a first-round game in Champaign (16 teams were invited at that time), the Warriors jumped all over Chicago Von Steuben, leading 15-0 in the first quarter. Von Steuben came back to win the game, however. There were rumors swirling back home in Granite City after the tournament that the team had engaged in late night partying in Champaign, the night before the game. That's as good an explanation as any for their collapse after dominating the first quarter against the Chicago school.

One member of that team was Phillip. Although only a sophomore on that squad, his immense potential was undeniable. Could there be more hidden gems like Phillip from the wrong side of the tracks, walking the halls of Granite City High School, just waiting for an opportunity to perform?

"I think Andy was a pioneer in that sense," said his brother Robert Phillip, five years his brother's junior. "I don't think it was anything personal, but there certainly was a bias against athletes from Lincoln Place before he came along.

"Because of his personality and his ability, they saw what he could do and I think that opened up the doors for the rest of the kids from down there."

Leonard Davis, who captained Bozarth's first basketball squad at Granite City in 1928 and had returned to his hometown to teach and coach, believed there was un-mined gold across the tracks. Davis, who grew up on the so-called right of the tracks, developed a soft spot in his heart for the immigrant kids. Before joining the high school staff in 1935 as a vocational teacher, and assistant to Bozarth in basketball, football and track, Davis had taught briefly at Washington School, the elementary school serving Lincoln Place and West Granite.

"What I suspect happened is that Leonard Davis got involved and told Bozarth, 'Hey, there are some kids here that you should take a look at,' " Hagopian said. "I'm sure they talked about it. I promise you I wouldn't have been on that team if Leonard Davis hadn't come along.

"I didn't have a problem with Bozarth, but all the kids loved Leonard. He was my man. He started at the elementary school with us and he had a soft spot in his heart for the immigrant kids. He saw us develop; he knew what was going on."

Bozarth is revered in Granite City to this day, but how much of an actual tactician he was is open for debate. Granite City obviously had some very good seasons, but there were some bad ones as well.

"I would say all the guys liked him and certainly respected him," Hagopian said. "I don't know that he always put the best players on the floor, but he did (in 1940).

"He was as good a coach as the players he had to work with."

Bozarth actually did two stints at Granite City. In basketball, he unquestionably did his best work from 1927 through 1941.

Bozarth won six conference titles in basketball and placed second five times in his first 14 seasons. He won five regional and two sectional titles.

His greatest year in football was the immortal "Happy Warriors" team of 1928. That team was undefeated and won the Southwestern Illinois Conference title as did Granite City's 1930, 1932 and 1936 teams.

That 1928 team was regarded by many as the best in Illinois that year although there would be no state playoffs for another 50 years. That team, which outscored its conference opponents, 146-12, featured the "Unholy Three" of fullback Tommy Wilson and halfbacks Bud Colin and Ed Rich.

Bozarth shocked Granite City when he left teaching and coaching in the spring of 1941, months before the outbreak of World War II, to become a physical instructor for the Air Force. He returned to Granite City in 1947 and coached basketball six more seasons, eventually retiring from coaching after his 1953 team went 3-21. The records for his first stint at Granite City are incomplete, but in the second stint he didn't have a winning season and was 49-99.

Bozarth, who possessed a ready and dry wit, could never be accused of hogging the spotlight from his players. By today's standards, Bozarth would be considered almost reclusive because of his penchant for avoiding publicity.

According to a story published in the Granite City paper shortly after the state title, Bozarth never allowed himself to be photographed with any of his teams in his first 12 years at the school.

"What do you want me for?" Bozarth was quoted in the story as telling the paper's photographer, Joe Blessman. "It is the boys. They did it. Leave me out of this."

But in the fall of 1939, the season before the championship basketball season, Bozarth relented and agreed to be photographed with his football team. Surprisingly, Bozarth picked this team – the last-place team in the Southwestern Illinois Conference, of all teams – for his coming out party.

"What's the idea, Coach?" asked the team's halfback, Clarence Hoy. "Do you figure 13 years is your lucky number?"

Without missing a beat, Bozarth replied, "No, but you boys are so terrible, you need someone to stand up with you."

When the seasons changed from football to basketball in late 1939, Blessman was assigned to take a pre-season publicity shot of the basketball team. The basketball players, apparently feeling the snub of Bozarth's perennial avoidance of their team photo shoot, "kidnapped him" as the story goes, and held him while Blessman did his work. The picture shows George Gages, the biggest boy on the team, firmly holding the arm of his uncomfortable coach.

Biting comebacks weren't Bozarth's only weapon of retort. Once, after losing a game to one of his former players who had ascended to the coaching profession, Bozarth reached into his bag of Whitman quotes for a response.

"I am the teacher of athletes," Bozarth repeated a Whitman quote. "He that by me spreads a wider breast than my own, proves the width of my own. He most honors my style who learns under it to destroy the teacher."

Although Bozarth was known as a keen competitor, he never lost sight of the fact that he was an educator first. He once expounded his thoughts on the mission of athletics.

"First, to teach boys how to be happier and healthier; second, to teach boys in such a way that they will become better and more responsible citizens...Education is not an end in itself, but must contribute to good life."

Bozarth's principles of good sportsmanship were put to a test early in his days at Granite City when his football team lost a game on what was perceived to be a very shaky call by an official. The story goes that irate Granite City fans gathered outside the team's dressing room, demanding to know what Bozarth planned to say to the offending official.

Someone in the crowd apparently said. "Aren't you going to tell that guy off, Byron?"

He replied, "No, I am not. I think he made a mistake, but I think my quarterback made three. Why blame the official any more than my quarterback?"

Granite City High School song
written by Mrs. Leila "Shep" Bozarth

Here's a song for dear old Granite
Lift your voice and sing
Here's a cheer for dear old Granite
Shout it, let the echoes ring
Victory's our habit,
Let's win this game
But win or lose
We'll keep on fighting just the same
For school's what you make it...
Granite can take it
Fight, fight fight for Granite High

8. THE NATURAL MAN

Long before the word "superstar" became an integral part of the American sporting lexicon, Andy Phillip was the living embodiment of the word.

When he was called on to score, as he was with the famed University of Illinois "Whiz Kids," he scored in bunches. When he was needed to dish out assists, as he was throughout most of his stellar 11-year professional basketball career, he proved to be a most generous benefactor to his teammates.

And, when he was needed to do literally everything – score, rebound, pass, defend – as he was with the Happy Warriors, he gladly accepted his duties. Phillip, the only University of Illinois product to be enshrined in the Naismith Basketball Hall of Fame in Springfield, Mass., will always be known as a basketball player, but his athletic talents went far beyond.

He was such a gifted athlete that at age 14 he was signed to a professional baseball contract by a St. Louis Cardinals scout, who happened to be watching a semi-pro game he was playing in against grown men. While at Illinois, Phillip played a summer for the Cardinals' AAA team in Winston-

Salem, N.C. Phillip even briefly tried his hand at football while at Illinois, and although he was a very good prospect at end, was talked out of it by his basketball teammates, who wisely understood what he meant to their team.

By all accounts, Phillip was as good a person away from the athletic fields as he was on them, a fact that speaks volumes about the man.

"Andy was such a humble person," said his widow, Corky Phillip. "I called him my star. He was a gentle and generous man. He was very patient with me and I needed that. He was so full of love."

Phillip's younger brother Robert remembers Andy in much the same way.

"Andy was just a compassionate and loving man," he recalled. "He was willing to help anybody, regardless of what it was. I remember him coming back to Granite City when he was playing professional ball and organizing the kids' basketball games over at Lincoln Place.

"He never forgot where he came from."

Phillip was as beloved by his teammates as he was by his family.

"Andy was on that 1938 team that went to the state tournament because they saw something in him," Hagopian said. "They must have sensed that he was going to develop into a real leader and a great player.

"Andy did everything for our team. He'd go inside and score, shoot from the outside, great defender and rebounder. He was just outstanding in every aspect of the game.

"Andy wasn't a real vocal leader, he wouldn't raise his voice to anyone. But you knew if you did something wrong because he would let you know. That's the kind of leader he was."

While Phillip was the acknowledged leader of that 1940 team, it didn't matter to him who scored the points. That was never clearer than on the final play of his high school career.

In the closing seconds of the state championship game, with Granite City and Herrin tied at 22, Phillip passed up a shot at winning the game, instead dribbling till he found reserve Ed Hoff open at the free throw line. Hoff, playing in place of the injured Hagopian, pivoted and started a drive to the hoop.

Hoff slipped and fell, but from the seat of his pants spotted Parsaghian cutting to the basket and connected with him for what proved to be the game-winning basket.

"Andy always said he was going to take the last shot, but he didn't think he had a good shot," Corky Phillip recounted her husband's tale. "Instead, he passed the ball to Evon, who made the winning basket. That's just the way Andy was, very unselfish."

Apparently University of Illinois coach Doug Mills, who was in attendance that night at Huff Gym where the Illini then played, liked what he saw of Phillip as well. Legend has it that Mills offered Phillip a scholarship on the spot and Phillip accepted.

It was a pact that neither man ever regretted. Phillip was the lynchpin of the Whiz Kids, perhaps the greatest team in University of Illinois history, and

Mills was rewarded with back-to-back Big Ten titles in Phillip's first two seasons in Champaign.

The Whiz Kids, who included sophomores Phillip at guard, Ken Menke, who had starred for Dundee against Granite City in the 1940 state tournament at forward, Jack Smiley of Waterman, Ill. at forward, and Gene Vance of Clinton, Ill., at guard, burst onto the scene for the 1941-42 season. They joined holdover players, centers Arthur Mathisen and Victor Wukowits, who had helped the 1940-41 squad compile a 13-7 record.

It was heady times for the Illini as they won back-to-back Big Ten titles for the first time in school history, going 13-2 (18-5 overall) in 1941-42 and 12-0 (17-1 overall) the following season.

Illinois lost in the first round of the fledgling eight-team NCAA Tournament to Kentucky, 46-44, in 1942 and inexplicably was not invited to the still eight-team invitational in 1943. Illinois' only loss that season was a 41-31 decision to Camp Grant at Rockford, Ill.

The Illini were an offensive juggernaut in those two seasons, averaging 58 points per game, while most teams of that era were averaging in the low 40s. Phillip led the team in scoring, averaging 10.1 points in 1942 and 16.9 points in 1943.

In the team's 92-25 pummeling of the University of Chicago in his final game before departing for active duty with the U.S. Marines Corps, Phillip poured in 40 points, which was an unheard of number in those days and stood as the University of Illinois' single game scoring record for 20 years until Dave Downey scored 53 points against Indiana in 1963.

Phillip attempted 54 goals in that contest, which still stands as an Illini record. It is the longest-standing mark in the Illinois record book.

As jubilant as the Illini were on that night, there was a dark cloud hanging over their near-perfect season. By this time, World War II was in full swing. The team disbanded after that game, with all five starters – Phillip, Smiley, Vance, Menke and Mathisen – enlisting in the armed forces.

Phillip enlisted in the Marines and was assigned to the Pacific Theatre. He saw fierce action in one of the bloodiest battles of the Pacific – Iwo Jima.

"Andy said he didn't think he'd ever get off that island alive," Corky Phillip said. "I told him that "God saved him for me."

Phillip and his three classmates, Menke, Smiley and Vance, all returned safely and resumed their careers three years later for Mills' final season at Illinois, the 1946-47 season. While they were still a fine team – 14-6, 8-4 in the Big Ten – the magic that was the Whiz Kids was left on the battlefields of Europe and the Pacific.

Despite being gone for three years, the Whiz Kids were far from forgotten by Illinois' student body and fans. A crowd of 7,785, the largest crowd in Illini basketball history at that point, jammed Huff Gym to the rafters for their homecoming game on Dec. 6, 1946.

The original Whiz Kids pounded poor Cornell, their unwitting dupes, 49-13, in the first half and watched from their seats on the bench as their replacements polished them off, 87-39.

9. MR. POPULARITY

It didn't happen overnight, but Phillip's game was to take a dramatic turn when he left the University of Illinois to embark on a long career in professional basketball.

Perhaps it was a natural evolution of his game conforming to the realities of the professional style, which saw such players as George Mikan and later Bob Pettit, Wilt Chamberlain and Bill Russell dominate the lanes. At 6-3, Phillip could score inside or out while at Illinois and left there as the Big Ten's all-time leading scorer. But the NBA, even in its infancy, was a tough place to build a scoring average, especially in the paint.

Phillip entered the league as a big scorer, averaging in double figures in his first seven seasons in pro ball, first with the Chicago Stags, then with the Philadelphia Warriors and Fort Wayne Pistons. But as the league super-sized itself in the lane, Phillip gradually morphed himself from scorer into playmaker.

In the 1954-55 season, Phillip's scoring average dropped below double figures for the first time in his career at 9.6 and it declined every year thereafter.

But as Phillip's scoring average dropped, his assists per game average took flight. That made Phillip a very popular man with his teammates and may have prolonged his career and gotten him a World Championship ring.

"Getting the ball to my teammates made me a popular guy on the team," Phillip once said of his pro career. "Most of the time I'd rather make a good pass than hit a shot.

"In pro ball I got into playmaking and I stuck with it. I enjoyed making a good pass."

Phillip twice led the NBA in assists and in the 1951-52 season with the Warriors, he became the first NBA player to reach the 500-assist plateau, notching 555 for the season.

Considering Phillip's contemporaries were ball-handling magicians, Bob Cousy and Dick McGuire, his ability to get to the 500-assist plateau first was no small feat.

"People were always comparing Andy to Cousy and McGuire," said Fred Scolari, who roomed with Phillip when they were teammates with the Pistons. "To me, they were totally different. McGuire wasn't much of a scorer but was a very good passer. Cousy was a good passer, but attempted a lot more shots than Andy or McGuire.

"Andy was the steadiest of the three. He was not flashy. He made the simplest pass, but the best pass, the easiest pass under the circumstances. He was just a steady guy who made everybody around him better."

Phillip's unselfish attitude was what made him so alluring to then Boston Celtics general manager and coach, Red Auerbach, perhaps the shrewdest judge of basketball horseflesh in the history of the game.

After the 1955-56 season in which Phillip had averaged just 5.8 points per game, he decided to retire from basketball. But a phone call from Auerbach during the off-season reminded Phillip that he already missed the game and tempted him into becoming the final piece in what would be the Celtics' first NBA title.

"At the end of the 1955-56 season, I was ready to quit," Phillip said in an article published in the January 2002 edition of Basketball Digest. "The game had been very good to me and it just seemed like a good time for me to retire. I had put together some good years, and although I thought I still had a few seasons left in me, I figured it was time to say goodbye to the Fort Wayne Pistons, retire, and get on with my life.

"That was until I got a call from Red Auerbach. He called me up out of the blue one day during the off-season, telling me that the Celtics needed some help, that he liked me and wanted me to come play on the Celtics. He told me how Frank Ramsey was in the service and Bill Russell, who they just had drafted, wouldn't be eligible until after the Olympics.

"Let's just say that Auerbach must have had a way with words because as our conversation continued, I realized that I already had started to miss basketball. To make a long story short, he pretty much talked me into it. He arranged a trade with Fort Wayne and there I was, wearing a green uniform the next season when camp opened up.

"Part of the reason I was tempted to come out of retirement and join the Celtics was because they had a good chance of winning it all that year. They had been a very good team for several years, but now they were really starting to build something. Anyone could see that."

Phillip's role would be to back up Cousy and Bill Sharman at guard. That was fine with him.

"They always had a great backcourt with Bob Cousy and Bill Sharman. Those guys were magic with the ball. But then they added Ramsey and Tommy Heinsohn and Jim Loscutoff and Arnie Risen. They suddenly had the makings of a really strong team. Then you add Russell to the mix, and well, you've got a championship-caliber club.

"As the third guard on the team, I was a backup to Cousy and Sharman that year, and that was that. I had been a starter for most of my career up until that point, but I knew my role on the Celtics and I accepted it."

Despite coming off the bench, Phillip played a large role in the Celtics' first World Championship, in what would be a run of nine titles in 10 years and 11 in 13 years. He averaged 4.4 points and 2.5 assists in backing up Cousy and Sharman. Boston got its title with a 125-123 overtime victory over the St. Louis Hawks in Game 7 of the championship series and Phillip scored five points in the final game.

"No one mentioned the word 'championship' in the locker room," Phillip said later. "Not even the coaches did. We knew it was important and didn't need to be reminded.

"We didn't celebrate like they do today. We just went back to the locker room. Nowadays everyone wants a ring. Back then, we went back and got a soda."

Phillip came back for one last curtain call in 1957-58, but it was a downer. The Celtics lost the title to the Hawks in six games, and Phillip was relegated to a minor role, averaging career lows in scoring (3.4 ppg.) and assists (1.7).

"I knew it was time then," Phillip said.

But what a run it had been. Phillip left behind an NBA legacy of five All-Star games, a World Championship, a scoring average of 9.1 points per game, a rebound average of 4.4 per game and an assist average of 5.4 per game over 11 seasons.

"Andy hated to lose and he was a great competitor," said his teammate at Fort Wayne, Red Rocha. "He was an intelligent player, one of the smartest."

10. THE TEAM

Andy Hagopian spent his winter of 1938-39, his sophomore year at Granite City High School, sitting on the bench of the Granite City junior varsity basketball team.

"I guess they didn't think I had it," he said. "I must have improved a lot between my sophomore and junior years.

"Did I consider not trying out for the team the next year? No way, what else was I going to do?

"If I quit, where would I be? Out on the street, that's where. I stuck it out and it turned out great."

It's that attitude that made the Granite City Happy Warriors the champions they proved to be in 1940. While they played other sports – Phillip and Eftimoff both excelled at football and baseball – basketball was their passion.

From their days as youngsters at the Lincoln Center, where they learned about the game and each other, all they ever wanted to do was play basketball for Granite City High School. While Phillip was the team's undisputed star and leader, it was basketball by committee, the way the game was meant to be played.

Team. Team. Team.

The Happy Warriors' all-for-one attitude started from the top. Phillip, despite being the team's undisputed star and captain, was the ultimate team player. He finished second in the Southwestern Illinois Conference scoring race in 1940, to Collinsville's Levo Dallape. Phillip scored 185 points in 14 conference games that season (13.2 points per game), more than anyone had ever scored in the conference before, but Dallape trumped that with 235 (16.8).

Bozarth said after the season that Phillip's unselfishness was largely responsible for the team's success.

"Phillip sacrificed the scoring championship this season for team play," Bozarth would say after the season. "Rather than win the honor, he played along with his mates and that's the reason we had such a fine season."

As on any team, there was competition for playing time. But the players generally seemed to accept their roles without bitterness or rancor.

"There was rivalry and there was competition for playing time, just like there is on any basketball team," Hagopian said. "But there were no cliques or factions. All of us from Lincoln Place had known each other since we were kids and we were all friends. And, we got along great with the guys who weren't from down there, too.

"It was clear who the players were and what their roles were. Coach Bozarth set his starting lineup at the beginning of the season and these five were established.

"There was no friction. As long as we were capable, that was our position. People seem so amazed that because we were so many different nationalities that we all got along so well, but believe me, we were very well assimilated."

One thing everyone in Granite City knew at that time was that Phillip was the team's "horse" and if the Happy Warriors were to go anywhere it would be while riding on Phillip's strong back. At 6-3, Phillip was a raw-boned kid who was as equally deadly with his two-handed set shot as he was slicing to the hoop or positioning himself for offensive putbacks.

By all accounts, Phillip was as modest as he was gifted. He wasn't a vocal leader or one who would use his position as the team's undisputed star to criticize a teammate, but there is no question that Phillip, who had been a starter on the Granite City team since his sophomore season, was THE man.

"Andy wasn't that vocal but he was our leader," Hagopian said. "His leadership came through his performance and he did perform."

Phillip's brother Robert concurs with Hagopian's assessment of his brother.

"Andy just loved the game. He very seldom got angry with anybody, let alone his teammates. And if he did, he wouldn't talk about it."

While Phillip was the unquestioned star of the team, the only other player on the team with Phillip's raw athletic ability was the happy-go-lucky Parsaghian. Although standing just 5-11, Parsaghian was a force inside because of his phenomenal leaping ability. He was clearly the team's No. 2 scoring option and, especially early in the 1939-40 season, led the team in scoring on many nights.

"Evon was the best jumper on the team, even better than Andy," Hagopian said.

"He had the kind of jumping ability that you see of a lot of today's black players," Markarian added.

But while Parsaghian was physically gifted, he wasn't as dedicated to training as he should have been. Although he was the second leading scorer on the squad, he would often be the first player to be substituted for by Bozarth because he would tire out quickly.

"Evon was a very capable player, but he just didn't take care of himself," Hagopian said. "He'd tire easily on the court. He'd be great for short spurts but then he'd have to come out because he wasn't in condition to play the whole game. The starters would pretty much play the whole game except for Evon, because he'd be huffing and puffing out there.

"Evon was a good-time boy. He just lived a different life. He was a very handsome guy and got along really well with the girls...he played the field.

Parsaghian's sister Isabel Vartan confirmed her brother's success with the young ladies.

"I remember one time a whole group of girls in a car came to our house looking for Evon," Vartan said. "My mom didn't like that one bit."

Hagopian wished that Parsaghian had been as attentive to his training as he was to the ladies.

"Evon played a big part in our success and he had the talent to be an exceptional player, but his living habits prohibited that from happening. I think he could have been the equal of Andy if he had disciplined himself.

"But you'd see him before a game eating one of those little cherry pies or a banana."

Probably the next most talented player on the team was the lumbering Gages, who at 6-3, 220 pounds gave the team an inside presence. It took Gages a few weeks into the season to establish himself as the team's top post player, but once he emerged from his personal battle with Everett Daniels for the starting center spot, he consistently improved as the season went on.

Gages improved so greatly during the season that he was offered a basketball scholarship by Bradley University. He had to turn it down, however, because he was his family's lone provider and went to work as a machinist after high school.

"They were poor people," said Gages widow Helen of his family. "His mother was a housewife and his father was a blacksmith, who mainly repaired farm equipment.

"George was such a modest man. Later in life, we had a new minister at church and one Sunday as we were leaving the church he said to George, 'My, you're a tall one. You must have played a little basketball in your day.'

"All George said was 'I played a little.' He never bragged about winning a state championship. He was just so proud of his team."

That's the way Hagopian remembered Gages, who was perhaps his best friend on the team.

"George was a quiet man, he didn't talk much," Hagopian said. "He was just very reserved in spite of his athletic abilities.

"He was such a nice, jovial man, a gentle giant, he was my protector in grade school. In fact he was too nice...I used to tell him to be more aggressive on the basketball floor."

Like Gages, "Huggy" Hagopian was a player who also improved steadily as the season progressed. He went from not being sure if he would make the squad at the beginning of the season, after languishing on the JV bench his freshman and sophomore years, to making the second-team all-state tournament squad.

"Honestly, it was very disappointing to me not getting into games when I was a freshman and sophomore," Hagopian said. "I thought I could play, but I guess the coaches didn't think so.

"If it hadn't been for Coach Davis, I probably never would have made the team my junior year and been on the team that won the state title. He was my champion.

"I didn't really have the background to be a starter on that team, but Coach Davis must have seen something and convinced Bozarth because I was a starter from the start of the season. I can't answer what happened because I think I was the same player I always was."

Like Gages, Hagopian hit his stride for the state title run.

"Up until the state tournament my whole role was to stay back on defense," Hagopian said. "I don't really know what happened at the state tournament – I just started scoring after scoring very little all season."

The team's fifth starter was Danny Eftimoff, who at 5-8 was an inch shorter than Hagopian, yet played forward for the state champions. Doing the dirty work was nothing new for the gritty Eftimoff, however, who was also the Happy Warriors' baseball catcher in the spring and football center in the fall.

"Danny was a good defensive player and he had that one spot that he loved to shoot from," Hagopian said. "We loved to get him the ball down there on the baseline where he could hit from about 18 feet out. We would try to maneuver the ball to get it to him down there.

"I wouldn't say Danny was an outstanding basketball player, but he was a very good all-around athlete. He was a very quiet guy. He could shoot from either side from the baseline – that was his spot."

Ebbie Mueller was the team's back-up forward who got to see the most action of any of the subs because he was the replacement for the oft-winded Parsaghian. Hoff seldom saw playing time, but he got his moment in the sun when he played most of the state championship game in place of the injured Hagopian.

Daniels, whose nickname was "Farmer," was perhaps the closest thing to an outsider that the team had. He earned his nickname because he was from a rural area outside of Granite City and he transferred into the school just before the season.

"He was a big farmer boy, about 6-feet-2," Hagopian said. "We didn't know too much about him before the season because he transferred in.

"He had some ability, but George beat him out. I know Daniels wasn't too happy about it, but he accepted it."

Markarian didn't join the team until the sectional tournament, replacing Earl Kunneman, who had the misfortune of suffering appendicitis late in the season. Markarian's best qualification was that he could shoot with either hand, a rarity for that era when shooting the two-handed set shot was standard procedure.

The 10th member of the squad was Sam Mouradian, just a freshman.

"Sam didn't get to play much and he wasn't too happy about it," Hagopian said. "But he was only a freshman. He had his day later on."

11. HOW THEY PLAYED THE GAME

There was the sort of chemistry with the Granite City starting five that comes from playing with each other for years and knowing each other's game intimately.

But Andy Hagopian and Evon Parsaghian, the team's two Armenian starters, shared something that even their closest friends, Andy Phillip, George Gages and Danny Eftimoff, knew nothing about – the Armenian language.

And, it was quite a weapon.

"Evon and I would talk to each other in Armenian the whole game," Hagopian said. "We'd set up plays. Our best play was when there was a center jump, usually at the start of the game.

"I'd tell him, "I'm going...*yes, gertam* in Armenian, or he would tell me he was going...always in Armenian. Our teammates didn't understand Armenian, but they knew what that meant.

"If Evon was taking a jump ball for example, I would look the situation over and then tell him in

Armenian, exactly what I was going to do. Nobody else knew what we were talking about.

"We used it in every game and we used it very much in the state tournament. I'd say we had about a 50 percent success rate. We'd catch the other teams napping quite a bit."

The straight-laced Bozarth, the man who didn't exactly welcome the immigrants with open arms to begin with, embraced this idea.

"I would say Coach Bozarth liked the idea a lot," Hagopian said. "In fact he championed the idea. He was favorably impressed. There were times when he would call for that play or a certain inbounds play where Evon and I talked to each other.

The other two Armenians on the team, John Markarian and Sam Mouradian, also spoke Armenian, but were seldom used in prime time. Almost every Armenian who lived in Lincoln Place at that time spoke the language fluently, either learning it from their parents or from classes at Lincoln Place.

"It's a very simple language and very logical alphabet," Hagopian said. "There is a letter assigned to each sound...like a letter for "sh," that you don't have in the English language."

Andy Phillip didn't understand much Armenian, but he certainly felt that the team's common backgrounds were a huge factor in their success.

"We all grew up together and played together all the time at Lincoln Place (Community Center)," Phillip was quoted as saying in a 1997 interview with Patrick C. Heston of the Granite City Press-Record.

"That made us a much better team than we would have been otherwise.

"We knew what the other person was going to do. We could anticipate each other's moves."

By 1940, the center jump after every basket had been eliminated, but it was still used for every possession dispute. The game was changing by 1940, but ever-so-slowly in Granite City. Defense and deliberate play were the trademarks of Bozarth's teams of that era.

While teams like Dundee, a squad that Granite City was to meet in the state quarterfinals and led by Phillip's future teammate at Illinois, Ken Menke, were playing the game at a break-neck pace, the Happy Warriors were content to walk the ball up the floor. The only fast-breaking the team did was when Parsaghian and Hagopian would work their Armenian mojo on unsuspecting opponents.

When Granite City got into its offense, it was all patterns and patience. Bozarth had four plays – "Mueller," "Eftimoff," "Ebbie" and "Evon" – each designed for one particular player to score, and the Warriors were drilled to run them instinctively. Surprisingly, none of the plays were called "Andy" or "Phillip" but perhaps Bozarth felt that might have been a bit too obvious.

The Happy Warriors averaged just 38.4 points per game in their championship season. That was a little bit below average, even for that era, but considering they held their opponents to just 26.0 points per game, it worked out well.

"We played a slow style offense, the kind of style Bozarth liked," said Phillip in the same Granite City Press-Record interview. "We always felt that if a team pressed us and put the pressure on us to pick up the pace, that it would give us some problems."

The play that was called most often was Phillip's and with good reason. Based on box scores located for 20 of the team's games that season, Phillip led the team with a 13.8 average.

"Andy and Evon were the first two options," Hagopian said. "They could both take it to the hoop or shoot from outside."

Parsaghian, who carried the team early in the season, was the No. 2 option with an 8.75 points per game scoring average. Hagopian and Gages, both of whom came on late, averaged 6.2 and 4.9 points per game respectively in the games for which box scores were found.

Everett Daniels, the team's backup center, had a 2.3 point per game average which was slightly better than Eftimoff's 1.75. There was never a doubt who the team's main man was, however.

"Andy Phillip was the greatest basketball player I ever saw," Hagopian would say in later years. "No one else was even close.

"And, he was at his best in the state tournament. He carried us throughout the tournament and the championship game. In fact, he carried us all season long."

Dick Yates, who was a junior on the 1938 Granite City team that qualified for the State Finals when

Phillip was a sophomore, thought this of his ex-teammate in the Press-Record article.

"Andy Phillip was one of those rare players, who was always at the right place at the right time," Yates said. "He wasn't exceptionally fast on the floor, but what he had was great basketball savvy.

"He had a great floor sense and game sense. That, to me, was his strong point. And he had a good shot, good reflexes and reacted well and correctly to everything that happened."

In assessing his own game, Phillip had this to say: "I think what made me a good basketball player was that I had a good sense of, a good feel for the game. I think that was most important.

"Then I could jump, I could shoot, I could dribble – and shoot with both hands. I also had good vision, good instinct and was a playmaker."

Phillip credited the training and coaching he received from Bozarth for his long and celebrated basketball career.

"Those days in Granite City were the formative days of my life," Phillip said to the Press-Record in one of his final interviews. "It was in high school, playing for Coach Bozarth that I learned the fundamentals of the game of basketball.

"Fundamentals were then, are now, and always will be, the secret to success in basketball.

"You couldn't play for Bozarth and not be fundamentally sound. He demanded it. That enabled me to be successful at higher levels later on."

Bozarth also was a stickler for floor balance. One of the reasons opponents averaged just 26 points per game that year was because Granite City didn't give up easy baskets.

"Coach Bozarth was very big on court balance and I was the guy he wanted to stay back to make sure the other team didn't get any easy baskets," Hagopian said. "(Phillip) was the other guard, but he couldn't stay back because he was so good at driving to the basket.

"Somebody had to stay back on defense and that was my job. Andy and I were the guards and Andy's job was to drive to the basket and score, so staying back was my job. I didn't really start scoring until the state tournament.

Defensively, Granite City played strictly man-to-man defense.

"There was no such thing as a zone for us," Hagopian said. "Our two guards would take the opponent's two guards, our forwards would guard their forwards and George would guard their center.

"There was no scouting or anything like that going on. It was strictly guard your man."

As mild-mannered a man as he was off the court, Gages was a tiger on the boards.

"He scored most of his points on rebounds," Hagopian said of his buddy Gages. "Sometimes I wished George was more aggressive...he was such a nice guy. But he was very good inside there."

Gages would say later in life: "The baskets I made were the baskets (Phillip) missed usually. It took them a long time to get around me. I cleared my own way."

While most states employ three referees for varsity high school games in this era, one official was used for the games in those days and needless to say, one man couldn't see everything that was going on.

"(Opponents) would actually grab the back of my pants to hold me down," Gages said. "There was only one referee then and he couldn't see everything.

12. HAROLD AND "LITTLE BETSY"

If "Coach" was another way of saying Byron Bozarth in Granite City in 1940, "Manager" was a good pseudonym for Harold Brown. No matter what the season – fall, winter or spring – Brown was Granite City's most indispensable performer.

Whether it was officiating a junior varsity game for no pay, rebounding Andy Phillip's free throws late into the night, setting up track hurdles or wheeling about his home-made combination towel/water bottle contraption dubbed "Little Betsy," Brown was the man for the job. Even now, almost 70 years after his unfaltering service to the Granite City athletic programs, it is clear why Brown volunteered his services.

"I did it for Byron," Brown said. "I would do anything for that man, I admired him so much. We were very close."

The story goes that Bozarth sought out Brown as a freshman to help him with a track meet because Brown was familiar with the markings on the track that designated where hurdles were to be placed and baton exchange zones. That was the beginning of a close-knit relationship that was to overlap into football and basketball seasons as well.

"Byron loved to work with young people and he cared greatly for them," Brown said. "He was a very intelligent man, a great guy and we were very close.

"When he passed away it was a very sad day for me because I thought he was a great man. He got along with all the kids and he never kicked anybody off the football or track teams. I never heard him run anybody down.

"He was someone I always respected and appreciated."

It's quite certain that the feeling was mutual. If Andy Phillip was the hardest working member of the basketball team, then Brown was probably the second hardest worker.

"I can tell you why Andy Phillip was such a great basketball player," Brown said. "It's because he worked harder than anybody else.

"Andy would stay after practice every night and shoot free throws until he made 50 in a row without a miss. I know this because I was there rebounding for him. I was in charge of the equipment and I couldn't go home until everything was put away.

"Some nights Andy would make 50 right away and I could go home at 6. Other nights we'd be there till 8 o'clock."

"Andy's attitude was 'You're never going to beat us... you might as well quit.' That was the type of person he was – not cocky, or arrogant, but confident."

Brown said while Phillip was the undisputed leader of the team, there was never any back-biting or jealousy.

"The starters all knew each other so well, they got along like clockwork," Brown said. "They all respected each other and even those guys who weren't from (Lincoln Place) – they were all in harmony. And nobody was ever jealous of Andy – they all knew he was fantastic.

"You talk about cliques on a team. Well, that whole starting five was a clique. They all got along. They played together, they laughed together, they liked each other. To them, it didn't matter who scored the points.

"It was those five guys from Lincoln Place that won the championship for us. They knew each other inside and out."

Brown had the best seat in the house for Granite City basketball games, but he was far more than just an observer. He was an innovator as well, the mastermind behind "Little Betsy," which headed a laundry list of superstitions and quirks shared by the Happy Warriors.

Little Betsy was a contraption designed and built by Brown that was basically a towel rack/water bottle holder on wheels. It also had a bicycle horn attached that each player would squeeze for luck as they exited their locker room before a game.

"Little Betsy" gained notice at the state tournament, although not in a positive way, when Brown wheeled it on to the Huff Gym floor only to spill water everywhere. The contraption was banned from the floor from that point on.

"'Little Betsy,' was just a little thing I made for the team," Brown said. "It had a holder for the water bottles and you could hang the towels on it. Every time we had a time out, I'd wheel it out there on the floor."

For a team that claimed not to be superstitious, the Happy Warriors had a boatload of superstitions. In addition to the team's quirkiness surrounding "Little Betsy" there was also the sock thing.

"I won't mention any names but there were some guys who wouldn't change socks until we lost," Brown said.

Considering the team had a 12-game winning streak, from Dec. 27, 1939, when the Happy Warriors beat Mattoon in the first round of the Mount Vernon Christmas Tournament, through Feb. 2, 1940, when they finally lost at Collinsville, that's a long time to go wearing the same sweaty socks.

There were also superstitions just for road games. While there was no assigned seating, each player sat in the same seat for every bus ride.

And, every bus ride included the entire team joining in and signing the popular song of that era – "You are my sunshine, my only sunshine."

"I think Farmer Daniels started that," Hagopian said. "I can still hear that song...'you are my sunshine, my only sunshine.'"

There were individual superstitions as well. Ebbie Mueller took his lucky horseshoe with him to every game and he prominently displayed the lucky shoe in every picture taken of the squad.

Hagopian, who now downplays the idea of superstitions, told a different story when he was interviewed for a newspaper article just after the Happy Warriors won the state title.

"I had only one superstition at the tournament, but it seemed to work," Hagopian is quoted as saying. "Before each game, Mr. Habekost (Granite City teacher) brought me a little penny charm and told me how many baskets to make. Each time I made as many baskets as he told me."

"Little Betsy" was just part of the unusual, some would say bizarre, setting that was Granite City basketball of that era. The team played its games on an auditorium stage, not an uncommon occurrence in those days, because the auditorium had a greater seating capacity than the school's gym at that time.

Obviously, it wasn't an ideal situation for either the fans or the players. There were plenty of blind spots on both ends of the floor and players always had to consider the consequences of landing in the orchestra pit if they dove for a loose ball.

For all its inconveniences, the auditorium facility gave the Happy Warriors one heck of a home court advantage. In their championship season, they were 11-1 at home, somehow losing a non-conference match-up with lowly Gillespie, 41-39, in their second-to-last game of the regular season.

The auditorium was able to accommodate 2,200 fans according to reports from that time and it certainly filled to capacity for big games, especially with arch-rivals Wood River and Collinsville. Conspicuous by their absence, however, were the parents of most of the players from Lincoln Place.

"My parents never got to see me play a basketball game until the following season when Coach Bozarth was nice enough to let them ride with him when we played in the Mount Vernon Tournament," Hagopian said. "Even then, they didn't understand it. To them, basketball was just a game, something you do for fun. What they understood was hard work.

"Most of (Lincoln Place residents) were not economically or socially geared to basketball. It cost money to go watch the games.

"I don't believe many of them knew what was really transpiring that season. Even me...I didn't know it was that big a deal until we won it, years later.

"As far as we knew, we were just playing basketball. That's just something we'd always done."

Ebbie Mueller (far right, seated) always kept his lucky horseshoe close at hand as shown in this photo taken shortly after the Happy Warriors' 24-22 victory over Herrin in the 1940 Illinois State Championship game. Seated left to right are: Dan Eftimoff, Andy Phillip, Evon Parsaghian, John Markarian and Mueller. Standing: Coach Byron Bozarth, George Gages, manager Harold Brown, Everett Daniels, Ed Hoff, Sam Mouradian and Andy Hagopian.

The Happy Warriors were the toast of Granite City after their stunning success in Champaign. Part of the celebration included the team dancing a jig in front of the high school. From left are manager Harold Brown, Everett Daniels, Dan Eftimoff, Evon Parsaghian, Andy Phillip, Andy Hagopian, George Gages, Sam Mouradian, John Markarian, Ed Hoff and Ebbie Mueller.

The offical team composite photo of the Granite City Happy
Warriors, 1940 Illinois State Champions.

Andy Phillip pauses to savor the moment after Granite City wins the state title in Huff Gym.

Moline's Edsel Gustafson gets a lesson in post defense as George Gages (left) has position and Andy Phillip (47) and Evon Parsaghian (50) prepare to double team in semi-final state tournament action.

Gritty Danny Eftimoff did the dirty work for Granite City
in baseball, football and basketball. (Courtesy of Queenie
Elieff).

The last four surviving members of the 1940 Granite City basketball team shared their final reunion in 2003. From left: John Markarian, Ed Hoff, Andy Hagopian and George Gages (seated in front). (Courtesy of Helen Gages).

Byron Bozarth was the model family man. Here he spends quality time with his wife Leila (Shep), daughter Megan and the family collie. (Courtesy of Queenie Elieff).

Andy Hagopian was the smallest player on the floor most nights, but played a huge role in Granite City's success with his slick ballhandling and solid defense.

The starting five – (from left) George Gages, Danny Eftimoff, Andy Hagopian, Evon Parsaghian and Andy Phillip – ham it up with their state championship trophy at team's 40-year reunion in 1980. (Courtesy of Queenie Elieff).

The Lincoln Place Center – or "The Clubhouse" as it was affectionately known – as it appears today at 822 Niedringhaus Ave. in Granite City. (Melissia Ward photo).

13. BEWARE THE "TERRIBLE TURKS"

Keep in mind the words political and correctness were probably never used side by side in sentence form until the 1980s. Also, keep in mind lawyers, and the ACLU in particular, had more important matters to adjudicate in 1940.

Sensitivity training in 1940? Yeah, sure.

But still you have to wonder what Byron Bozarth, an erudite and well-educated man, was thinking when he referred to his 1939-40 basketball squad as his "Terrible Turks." It was just a throw-away line to a reporter from the Granite City Press-Record, but given the fact that he had on his roster at the beginning of the season, four Armenians and two Macedonians – both nationalities historical enemies of the Turks – it is a bit mind-boggling.

That would be roughly akin to a basketball coach of a team dominated by Jewish players in 1970, 25 years after the end of the Holocaust, calling his team his "Horrible Huns." But 1940 was a different time and many would say a better time...certainly a less complicated time. It was a time when teachers ruled their classrooms with an iron fist and coaches were dictators in their own little fiefdoms.

With the exception of Andy Phillip, there were no indispensable players on the 1939-40 Granite City basketball squad. He and Dick Yates were the team's all-conference players in 1939 and Phillip was designated team captain for the 1939-40 season after leading the previous team in scoring.

Evon Parsaghian also played a big role with the 1939 squad that finished 18-10 and won the Southwestern Illinois Conference championship, but otherwise, the other starting jobs were up for grabs. George Gages, now a junior, senior Danny Eftimoff and senior Ebbie Mueller, had all won letters the previous season and were expected to compete for starting jobs in 1939-40.

Also returning were lettermen Waldo Grigoroff and Clarence Hoy. Neither would be around at the end of the season because Granite City, at that time, practiced mid-year graduation and both graduated in January.

Also on the roster at the beginning of the season were Russell Long, Tony Georgeff, Otto Fisher, Delore Birmingham, Everett Daniels, Sam Mouradian, and Andy Hagopian. By the end of the season, only Daniels, Mouradian and Hagopian, among that group, would still be with the team.

Hagopian, who languished on the junior varsity bench as a sophomore, was barely mentioned in a pre-season assessment of the team.

A story in the Granite High World, the high school's paper, quoted Bozarth's assistant coach,

Leonard Davis as saying "this is the best freshman and sophomore bunch he's ever seen," and that "A," "B," "C" and "D" squads would be formed for the first time in the school's history. That meant "there won't be a boy dropped from playing."

Oddly enough not a word was written about how good the varsity might be. There was no indication in early December of 1939 that this was a team bearing any resemblance to a state champion contender.

The season opened Dec. 5, 1939, at home against Staunton, Bozarth's alma mater. According to the report in the Press-Record, the game was played before a packed house in Granite City's auditorium arena.

Led by Parsaghian's 17 points, the Happy Warriors pounded Staunton, 38-23. Granite City broke out to a 20-12 halftime lead and Bozarth was able to use 12 players in the contest. Phillip, somewhat surprisingly, was second in scoring to Parsaghian with nine points.

Bozarth was still searching for his team's soul four nights later when the squad ventured over to tiny Livingston for a Saturday night non-conference game. In what might be the low point of the early season for the team, Granite City was drummed by Livingston, 25-15.

"All I can tell you is that was the smallest gym, I've ever played in," Hagopian said. "There wasn't even a place for the spectators to sit. It was your classic "Band box" gym and I think we were probably a little bit in awe."

Granite City followed that with a full weekend of home games, their final home games of 1939, hosting East St. Louis on Friday, Dec. 15, in both teams' Southwestern Illinois Conference openers, followed by a non-conference rematch with Livingston on Saturday night.

The Warriors defeated East St. Louis, 36-20, and the Press-Record called it an "unexpected" victory. After a tight first half, Parsaghian and Phillip keyed Granite City's second half rally that saw the team pull away 20-12 after three periods.

According to the Press-Record's account, the turning point came as the first half ended and Phillips "whipped in a one-handed shot, nearly the length of the floor, to break an 8-8 tie." Again, Parsaghian led the team with 16 points and Phillip added 14.

The following night, the Warriors got their revenge on Livingston, 31-29, but as the score would indicate, it was anything but easy. According to the Press-Record's report, Phillip broke the deadlock with another long shot, "just as he had the night before."

After a fairly easy 42-30 non-conference victory at Benld on Dec. 19, the Warriors returned home for a Friday night contest with arch-rival Wood River. It was common knowledge that if Granite City was to repeat as Southwest Illinois Conference champions, it would have to find an answer for the Oilers and their star, Joe Astroth.

A crowd estimated at 1,500 packed Wood River's gym to witness the early season showdown. Oilers' center Harold Hudson sank a "long field goal" to give Wood River a 20-19 victory and a share of the conference lead with Collinsville.

"I had just made a free throw to make it 19-18 with a few seconds left and we thought we had the game won," said Hagopian. "But their hot player shot...it must have been from around the center jump circle, and they beat us by a point."

According to the Press-Record report, Granite City "had shown a slight edge all through the game." It was the first meeting of the season between these two rivals, but certainly not the last.

They would meet an unheard of four times during the season, splitting 2-2, with their fates intertwined in an unprecedented regional and sectional tournament situation.

Shrugging off the disappointment of losing at Wood River, the Warriors still had unfinished business in 1939 – the Mount Vernon Holiday Tournament. Perhaps the road loss to Wood River brought the team closer together because the Happy Warriors were soon to get a taste of the quality of basketball they were capable of playing.

Granite City bounced Mattoon, 45-39, in the first round of the 16-team tournament and followed that with a surprisingly easy 41-17 victory over Quincy in the quarter-finals. West Frankfort was no match in the semi-finals, falling 45-22, setting up a championship game of Granite City vs. Salem. Parsaghian set a tournament scoring record of 25 points in the West Frankfort victory.

Danny Eftimoff's last-minute free throw sealed Granite City's 32-29 victory over Salem in a tournament that the Press-Record said "included some of the most powerful quints in Illinois." Granite City led throughout the game, with 19-15 halftime and 30-23 third quarter leads.

Phillip, "whose reputation as a guard spread all over the district during the tourney," – according to the Press-Record, led the team with 14 points. Ray Blades, the manager of the St. Louis Cardinals baseball team, drove to Mount Vernon to witness the athleticism of his young prospect first-hand.

The Mount Vernon Register was impressed with Phillip as well.

"One of the greatest players ever seen in the Mt. Vernon gymnasium who paced the Happy Warriors to the 1939 championship of the Christmas Holiday tournament – was Andy Phillip of Granite City."

Parsaghian, who was the tournament's high scorer with a whopping 65 points in four games, added nine points in the title game. Both Phillip and Parsaghian were named to the all-tournament team.

Ironically, Wood River, which had won the tournament the previous year, was eliminated in the first round by Salem.

"When we won the Mount Vernon tournament... that's when we thought we might be a pretty good team," Hagopian would say.

14. BRING ON THE OILERS AND THE KAHOKS

Winning the Mount Vernon Holiday Tournament showed the Happy Warriors that they were more than just Andy Phillip and Evon Parsaghian, truly a team to be reckoned with in the Southwestern Illinois Conference.

At this point in the season, even qualifying for the state tournament was beyond their wildest dreams, but winning the conference championship was certainly a realistic goal, even after the disappointing one-point loss at Wood River before Christmas. The Southwestern Illinois Conference didn't have a great basketball tradition at that point in time, but it was certainly getting better with every year.

Collinsville started the conference's upwardly mobile trend by placing third in the state in 1937. Granite City continued the movement by qualifying in 1938, Phillip's sophomore season, although that team is best remembered for losing to Chicago Von

Steuben, 32-31, despite scoring the game's first 15 points.

Wood River, despite finishing behind Granite City in the conference in 1939, was impressive in the state tournament that year, advancing all the way to the semifinals and eventually finishing third. The Oilers were an impressive 27-7 in 1939 and certainly appeared to be the team to beat in 1940 with the return of high-scoring Joe Astroth.

But before Granite City could think about exacting revenge on the Oilers, it had a full weekend of games to open 1940, traveling to nearby Madison on Friday night and then hosting Collinsville and high-scoring Levo Dallape on Saturday night.

The Warriors had no trouble disposing of Madison, taking that game, 49-20, but Collinsville was quite another matter. A crowd estimated at 1,500 jammed into Granite City's Auditorium to witness the early season showdown.

Granite City led early in the contest, 7-3, but the Kahoks tied the game by halftime at 16-16. Collinsville led briefly in the third period, 22-20. Parsaghian's basket early in the third period put Granite City ahead, 28-26, and the Warriors would never trail again. Eftimoff and Phillip scored baskets and Hagopian added a free throw to nail down a 37-31 victory.

Phillip matched Dallape's 13 points in the head-to-head showdown of the conference's top two scorers, but Parsaghian was the difference with 10 points.

The two victories boosted Granite City's victory run to six straight and improved its conference record to 3-1. That record boosted the Warriors into a four-way tie for the conference lead with Collinsville, Wood River and their next opponent, surprising Edwardsville.

Playing at Edwardsville was a potential problem, but with Parsaghian (15 points) and Phillip (11 points) at the top of their games, the Tigers were no match for the charging Warriors.

Leading just 24-19 after three periods, Granite City put the game away by outscoring its hosts, 11-4, in the final quarter.

The team had a bit of a letdown the following night at home against lowly Belleville, managing just a 19-17 lead through three quarters. But Phillip (9 points) and Parsaghian (7 points) helped the Warriors pull away for a 27-22 victory.

Next up for Granite City was an easy portion of its schedule with three straight lower end of the conference teams – Alton and East St. Louis, on the road, and Madison at home. The Warriors took out Alton easily, 45-26, behind 12 points from Parsaghian and 11 from Phillip. Surprisingly, Everett Daniels, who had been quiet as the starting center all season, came alive with 10 points.

East St. Louis gave Granite City more game than it was expecting, trailing just 23-19 through three periods. But Phillip (14 points) and Parsaghian (13 points) scored all 10 of their team's fourth quarter points as the Warriors pulled away to a 33-20 victory.

Daniels reverted to his old ways, being held scoreless and Bozarth apparently was a bit concerned.

George Gages scored a basket in the contest off the bench, and will start to play an increasingly larger role from this point on.

Madison, which would go winless in the conference that season, was no match for the Warriors on their home floor, falling 40-23. Phillip scored 13, Hagopian had 9 and Parsaghian added 8, but perhaps the most notable numbers in the box score were Gages' 6 points. Daniels scored just 3 points and it was becoming apparent that Bozarth was beginning to see the center position as a job-sharing proposition, at least for the time-being.

The victory over Madison assured that Granite City's showdown with Wood River, scheduled for Feb. 2, would not be tarnished in any way. Both teams would enter the contest with 16-2 records and 8-1 marks in the Southwestern Illinois Conference.

Wood River's only loss in the conference was an early-season, 30-26 setback at Edwardsville. The Oilers' other loss came at the hands of Salem, the team Granite City beat in the Mount Vernon championship game, in the first round of that same tournament.

An article in the Granite City Press-Review previewing the contest, called the game a match-up of "two of the stoutest high school basketball teams produced by the Southwestern Illinois Conference in quite a few years." The anonymous writer of the story had no idea how right he would prove to be with that assessment.

Since a full house of perhaps 2,500 was expected for the contest, pre-game crowd control was to be handled by the schools' respective cheerleading squads.

"Cheerleaders of both schools will be stationed in the corridor prior to game time to direct fans to their own sections of the auditorium," the story said, while advising potential fans to arrive well before the anticipated tipoff of 8 p.m. "Wood River rooters will be seated on the left side and local fans on the right side.

"It will be a case of first-come, first served and those getting in late may have to stand or may not even be able to find standing room."

The story reminded fans that while Wood River had won the first meeting of the two teams in December, there might be a more important factor in Granite City's favor. The Happy Warriors hadn't been defeated on their unique home floor since 1937.

Ironically, the last team to beat the Happy Warriors on their home stage was none other than Wood River.

The crowd for the game was estimated in the next edition of the Press-Record to be 2,500, and as long as offense wasn't important to them, the fans certainly got their money's worth. In what was a near carbon copy of their earlier meeting, a 20-19 Wood River victory, Granite City turned the tables to win this time, 19-17.

Offense did not come easily to the Happy Warriors, who trailed most of the contest. Wood River, which led 12-10 at halftime, held Granite City scoreless in the third period as it opened a 14-10 lead.

Fortunately for the home team, Phillip was on his game. He scored 10 points in the contest, over half his team's total. Granite City outscored the visitors, 9-3, in the fourth quarter to pull out the victory.

The only other Warriors to score baskets were Parsaghian, Eftimoff and Gages. Hagopian added a pair of free throws and Daniels added one free throw.

Gages' basket gave Granite City its first lead of the contest at 17-16 and Phillip's final basket – "on a delayed dribble, he broke through for a snowbird," – iced the contest.

"The game was bitterly fought from the opening whistle and was one of the best defensive tilts seen on the local floor," reported the Press-Record. "Both teams used tight defensive tactics and the play was hard and fast. Fumbling and failure to make good on free throws were costly to both sides."

The bottom line is that at 9-1 the Southwestern Conference title was now Granite City's to lose. And that's exactly what the Warriors did a week later at Collinsville.

It wasn't pretty as Levo Dallape, who would go on to win the conference scoring title, scored 17 and the Kahoks prevailed, 41-28, beating Granite City for the fifth consecutive year in Collinsville. Phillip kept his team in the game with 14 points.

The teams battled to an 18-18 tie at halftime, but the Warriors' defense collapsed in the second half. According the Press-Record account of the game, Collinsville was 9 of 17 from the floor in the second half and 5 of 5 from the free throw line, outscoring the visitors, 23-10.

In reality, the final five games of Granite City's regular season were anti-climactic. Edwardsville, which had lost its top player to mid-year graduation, wasn't the team it was earlier in the season and fell, 49-20, in the Warriors' next outing.

The most notable thing about that game was that Gages started the contest and scored nine points while Daniels, the starter most of the season, was scoreless in limited action. It was 21 games into the season, but Bozarth had found his starting lineup.

Phillip scored 18, Hagopian had nine and Parsaghian added seven in the free-scoring Edwardsville contest.

The following weekend, Granite City scored two more victories – easily defeating conference foe Belleville, 42-21, on the road and then squeaking past Mount Vernon, 33-30. It was clear that a couple trends were forming as the team geared up for post-season play.

First, Parsaghian's scoring role was diminishing. The player who had been the Warriors' leading scorer early in the season, scored just nine points in the two victories as Phillip was asserting his role as the team's main man with 33 points.

The other trend was the emergence of the team's juniors, Hagopian and Gages. Hagopian had 17 points in the weekend's games while Gages, gaining confidence in his new role as starter, added 10 points while the player he replaced, Daniels, was held scoreless.

For some reason, Granite City played a second consecutive non-conference game with Gillespie the following Tuesday night. In a game in which no details were available, Gillespie prevailed 41-39. The most significant aspect of the loss was that it ended the Happy Warriors' three-year home winning streak.

Granite City claimed its share of the Southwestern Illinois Conference title with a 61-30 drubbing of Alton in its regular season finale. Phillip scored 20 points to give him a total of 185 in conference games.

While that broke the conference record of 178 points, set in 1938, it wasn't enough to top Collinsville's Dallape, who set a new standard with 215 points.

Phillip, Dallape and Wood River's Astroth were unanimous choices to the all-conference team. Parsaghian was named to the second team, missing the first team by one vote.

15. A BUMP IN THE ROAD

Before his athletic career was over, Joe Astroth would know the meaning of pressure. Playing eight seasons for Connie Mack's bottom-feeding Philadelphia/Kansas City Athletics, a de facto farm club for the New York Yankees of that era...now that was pressure.

But when Astroth, who played catcher in professional baseball for 15 years, stepped to the plate, he claims he never felt pressure.

"When I would go to the plate, I'd block everything out," he said. "All I saw was the pitcher and the ball. I didn't hear a thing.

"When I was in the on-deck circle, I would hear everything the fans were saying. But when I got to the plate, nothing..."

Astroth claims that his immunity to pressure was something he was always blessed with. In particular, he remembers converting two free throws with seconds left to play, that iced Wood River's 32-28 victory over Granite City in the finals of the 1940 Edwardsville Regional basketball tournament.

"To be honest, I couldn't have been more relaxed," Astroth said. "I knew how to make free throws. We shot them underhanded in those days and I always worked on my game.

"I was very confident. It was the same when I played baseball. I just didn't feel pressure."

By all rights, the Granite City story and 1940 season should have ended here. Call it fate, but for seven seasons – from 1936 through 1942 – the Illinois High School Association employed a very quirky rule. In a tournament that from Day One was a single elimination – a one-loss-and-you're-out affair – there was a brief change in the rules.

No team benefited from the rule more than Granite City, the ultimate Comeback Kids of Illinois high school basketball. Given the second chance, the Happy Warriors would become the first team in IHSA history to lose a game in the state tournament and wear the crown of champions at the end of the season.

When Cicero Morton High School pulled off the same feat in 1941, the powers that be at the IHSA decided that perhaps their second-chance plan wasn't such a great idea and ended it.

"They put the rule in effect because they were having so many upsets in the regionals that some of the best teams weren't making it to the state tournament," said Patrick Heston, a noted IHSA basketball historian and former sports reporter for the Press-Record. "I imagine they put an end to it because of what Granite City and Cicero Morton did.

"It paints the minds of people in a way about the championship. I'm sure there were plenty of complaints from the sports writers and coaches."

When he walked off the floor that night in Edwardsville, Astroth knew full well he had not seen the last of Granite City that season. Although his Oilers had beaten Granite City two of three times already that season, he knew there would be a fourth and final showdown the next week at the Highland Sectional.

"We were the cream of the crop in our league and it was the toughest league in the state at the time," Astroth said. "There were a lot of good athletes in that league.

"Sure, we thought we'd have to play them again, but that was fine. We figured we might as well settle it once and for all. We wanted that. It was our ticket to the state finals."

Having to beat the same team twice in a tournament might not sit well in some quarters, but Astroth and his Wood River teammates were the ultimate good sports in that regard. They may have questioned the fairness of the rule, but they didn't dispute it.

"When you look back, you can say it was a little unfair that we had to play them again, that they had a second chance, but that's the way it was set up back then," said Astroth, who after retiring from baseball would open a bowling establishment near Philadelphia with former A's battery mate Bobby Shantz. "I guess we didn't think you should be able to lose a game and win the state championship.

"But at the time we didn't think anything of it. We just wanted to play whoever they put in front of us."

Despite the intensity of the rivalry and the stakes that were involved between the Mississippi River schools, Astroth claims it was a "clean rivalry."

"We knew Granite City was a steel town and they knew Wood River was an oil town, but that was about it," Astroth said. "We knew they were immigrants, but we didn't know what nationality or religion they were and it didn't matter to us.

"All that matters is that they were good guys and good, clean competitors. We beat them in the regional but they were the better team in the sectional and that was that.

"I'll tell you this much. When they got to the state tournament, we were pulling for them. And, I'm sure they pulled for us the year before that."

Astroth played on the 1939 Wood River team that finished third in the state.

"They were a good representative of our league and our area and we wanted to see them win it all."

There certainly were no surprises in Granite City's first two games of the Edwardsville Regional. The Warriors' first two opponents were Southwestern Illinois Conference rivals, Madison and Edwardsville, two teams that they had beaten four times during the regular season by a combined score of 173-86.

The tournament games weren't any prettier. After leading 35-4 at the half, Granite City rolled to a 64-22 laugher over neighboring Madison in the regional opener. Evon Parsaghian and Andy Phillip combined for 25 points and Andy Hagopian and Everett Daniels were big helps with 12 and 8 points respectively.

Edwardsville was a bit more challenging, actually leading Granite City, 11-10, after a quarter. But the Warriors came back to lead, 29-20, at the half and pulled away, 41-22, after three periods.

No one on the Granite City side expected the cake walk to continue, but no one was really prepared for what would happen to them in the early stages of their third meeting with Wood River. Perhaps the team was flat because in essence it was a meaningless game with both teams assured berths in the Highland Sectional the following week, but the Warriors came out absolutely flat.

After playing to a 10-10 tie in the first period, Wood River broke the game open in the middle two periods, outscoring the Warriors, 21-7, in periods two and three.

"A foretaste of what was to come was indicated by the Oilers' uncanny flicking in of long shots," said the Press-Record's account of the first quarter. But if there was a silver lining for the Happy Warriors on this night, it was their performance in the fourth quarter.

Granite City limited the Oilers to two points in the period – Astroth's two late free throws – while scoring 11. Before he hit the late free throws, Granite City had rallied to within two points at 30-28.

Wood River may have relaxed a bit in the late going, but the box score shows that the Oilers used just seven players in the game, so apparently Granite City's rally wasn't against their reserves.

It may have been a small consolation, but the outcome also demonstrated that the Warriors could be competitive on a rare off night by Phillip. He scored just six points in the contest, while Gages and Parsaghian took scoring honors with 10 and 8 points respectively.

"We weren't happy about the way the game came out, but we were still alive and that's what counted," recalled Hagopian. "At that point they had beaten us twice and we had beaten them once, so we figured it was our turn to beat them in the sectional."

16. THE SECOND CHANCE

A spate of regional upsets in the early 1930s forced the Illinois High School Association to re-evaluate its tournament format. Interest in the state tournament was down because many observers felt that often the best teams had been eliminated in regional play.

To remedy that situation, the IHSA adopted a rule in 1936 that allowed both the regional champions and the runners-up to advance to sectional play. And, for the first few years, at least, the new format seemed to work.

In 1936, four runners-up won sectionals, including Johnston City which placed third in Champaign. Carbondale, Woodstock and Zeigler made it to state after losing in regional title games in 1937.

Glenbard, Milton and that ill-fated Granite City team made it to state in 1938, and Cicero Morton, Champaign, Gillespie and Peoria Woodruff turned the trick in 1939.

But no one was prepared for what happened in 1940 and it signaled the beginning of the end for the noble experiment. No less than seven of the 16 teams that advanced to the state finals that year had lost in the regional finals.

Incredibly, eventual state champion Granite City, runner-up Herrin and fourth-place Champaign, were all regional losers. Beardstown, Dundee, Salem and Taylorville also had picked up regional losses before winning their respective sectionals and advancing to the 16-team finals in Champaign.

When Cicero Morton equaled Granite City's feat in 1941, the dye was cast. It didn't help that the team Cicero Morton defeated for the title, Urbana, also had suffered a regional defeat.

Two consecutive blemished champions was not what the IHSA envisioned when it put the rule into effect. Only two regional losers – Cicero Morton and Olney – made it to state in 1942, but those two teams became the final two teams ever to make it to the state finals with a loss.

The IHSA had seen enough and the experiment was scrapped.

"They did away with it because what happened with Granite City and then Morton the following year," said IHSA basketball historian and former Press-Record sports writer, Patrick Heston. "There was a lot of complaining from the coaches and stories written about in the newspapers, about what a bad idea it was."

A story appearing in the Champaign News-Gazette after Granite City had won the state title, gathered opposing viewpoints from coaches from around the state. Springfield coach Mark Peterman, who had previously coached at powerful Canton, and won two state titles (1928 at Canton and 1935 at Springfield), apparently thought the second chance concept was a terrible idea.

"It's silly to crown a beaten team champion," Peterman said. "(Granite City) isn't even champion of its own regional, Wood River is."

Willard Larson, the man who replaced Peterman at Canton, took the opposing viewpoint.

"It's been six years since they started letting the runner-up advance," Larson said, after Granite City's state title. "They must have known that someday, one of them would win the title.

"To change it when one of them finally does win it, is not logical. That's as much as saying in the first place, 'Okay, fellows, you can go on to the tournament, but for goodness sakes don't win.'"

But in 1940, the Granite City basketball team thought it was anything but a bad idea. While none of the Happy Warriors were thinking state championship or even state finals heading into the Highland Sectional, it was at the very least a chance to play some more basketball.

And frankly, the Happy Warriors knew that their chances of at least making it to the sectional championship game were good. Jerseyville provided little resistance in the first game, falling, 64-27.

Livingston, a team that had pounded Granite City, 25-15, in the second game of the season, was up next after ousting tough Collinsville, 32-30. The Warriors had already avenged that early loss, beating Livingston, 31-29, a week after the first loss, but that decision was anything but convincing.

This time, Granite City left no doubt. The Warriors pummeled Livingston, 36-22, setting up a fourth game with Wood River, which had advanced to the sectional finals with a rather shaky 32-31 double overtime victory over O'Fallon.

Granite City, with Andy Phillip's game now reaching its full potential, Evon Parsaghian playing a strong supporting role and juniors Andy Hagopian and George Gages improving with every game, appeared to be playing its best basketball of the year. But Wood River was a team that had beaten the Warriors two out of three games, and denied them an outright conference title and a regional title.

According to the Press-Record account of the sectional, "crowds were so large that the gymnasium and auditorium couldn't accommodate them. It was estimated that several thousand fans were turned away during the three nights."

The sectional championship game started as everyone in the packed Highland gym expected it would. It was tight and it was played close to the vest.

Phillip scored the Warriors' first six points and Parsaghian hit "a one-handed shot from far out," according to the Press-Record account, as Granite City led narrowly, 8-6, at the end of a period.

Phillip, again, was the difference as Granite City began to assert itself in the second period. Hagopian's driving layup gave the Warriors their largest lead to that point, 13-9. Phillip's layup made it 15-9, and after a Wood River free throw, Phillip hit from outside to build the lead to 17-10.

Phillip missed another long shot, but Gages' rebound basket made it 19-10. Wood River scored another basket to make it 19-12 at the break.

As the game progressed into the second half, it became increasingly apparent that Granite City had surpassed Wood River as the superior team. The Warriors scored the first five points of the second half – a Gages' free throw, a Parsaghian tip-in and a layup by Hagopian off a Phillip assist – and the rout was on at 24-10.

As the teams headed into the fourth quarter, Wood River had rallied to cut into the lead, but still trailed, 28-17. Parsaghian's free throw made it 29-17, to open the fourth quarter but Joe Astroth retaliated with a basket for Wood River.

Wood River scored four straight to narrow the lead to 29-21, but that was as close as the Oilers would come. A turning point of sorts occurred when Astroth fouled out for "holding" Gages, who converted his two free throws.

With Astroth gone, the Oilers had no chance to come back. Hagopian scored off another Phillip assist and then added a free throw. Phillip's layup sealed the satisfying and decisive 36-22 victory.

Phillip was once again the undisputed star of the contest, scoring 14 points on six baskets and converting 2 of 2 free throw attempts. Hagopian added nine while Gages had seven and Parsaghian scored six.

They were the only Granite City players to score that night as Eftimoff fouled out in the fourth quarter and shared his playing time with Ebbie Mueller. Astroth led Wood River's attack with six points.

As satisfying as the victory assuredly was, the Press-Record cut the Warriors absolutely no slack. In the second paragraph of the story under the banner headline "GRANITE CITY CAGERS GO TO STATE FINALS," was this ominous reminder:

"Going to the state tournament is somewhat of a nervous ordeal for most high school youngsters and three (sic) years ago something of this sort caused the Warriors to lose a 15-point lead in the last half of their first game – and the game.

"Several hundred local fans are expected to accompany the team to Champaign this year and lend whatever moral support they can to the team's morale so that a repetition of the 1937 (sic) tragedy will not occur."

The story incorrectly referred to the disheartening collapse against Chicago Von Steuben as being in 1937 instead of 1938.

17. A TASTE OF CHAMPAIGN

What happened to the 1938 Happy Warriors when they got to Champaign is open to conjecture. But it's a hard fact that Granite City pummeled Chicago Von Steuben in the early stages of their first game at the state finals, leading 15-0 at the end of the first quarter and 24-11 at the half.

Unfortunately, the team imploded in the second half, eventually falling to Chicago Von Steuben, a predominantly Jewish school, 32-31. Von Steuben star Bernie Wexler, who would later play for DePaul University, led the comeback.

Granite City had a wonderful team that year with Kenny Parker, who would later go on to the University of Illinois and be the sixth man on the Whiz Kids teams, Kam Van Buskirk, Bill "Barrelhead" Harrison and Dick Yates. Andy Phillip and Evon Parsaghian were promoted from the sophomore team for the tournament.

Urban legend in Granite City has it that the Happy Warriors were so happy to be in Champaign that they stayed up late in their hotel rooms the night before the game and had nothing left in the tank for the second half on Thursday.

"I think they were just worn out," said Dick King, a close friend of Yates, who would later go on to be Granite City's class president in 1939. "I think they just stayed up late, not drinking or anything like that. They were just kids who liked to have a good time."

Parker denies that was the case.

"It was our first trip there and we were excited," said Parker, who was playing in his second season for Bozarth in 1938. "But if there were people staying up late and fooling around, I'm not aware of it.

"What happened was we only scored seven points in the second half and Von Steuben had a guy named Wexler who shot the eyes out of the basket in the second half. He was a good player and went on to play at DePaul.

"That's just the way basketball is. Sometimes you lose the momentum and the other team beats you. But we were all poor kids and we didn't do a lot of running around back then."

Whatever the truth is on that story, it's safe to say that expectations were modest at best for the Happy Warriors as they headed off to Champaign in 1940. For one thing, Granite City had no track record of winning, especially after the 1938 debacle.

And, for another, there were powerful teams like Dundee standing in its path. The Redbirds brought a 24-2 record to Champaign, and they had won the state title as recently as 1938.

But first up for Granite City was Streator, a team that finished just third in The Big 12 Conference of the north central region of Illinois. But at 22-8 the Bulldogs under Coach Lowell "Pops" Dale were big and said to be improving in the Press-Record's story previewing the first-round game.

According to the story, the biggest fear factor for the Warriors would be Streator's size. The Bulldogs apparently had three starters who stood 6-3 or taller and averaged 6-3 across their lineup. Granite City's starting five averaged 5-11, but played taller with George Gages, now firmly entrenched in the post, and good leapers Evon Parsaghian and Phillip crashing the boards.

The story concluded that since Streator had averaged 45.1 points during the regular season and that Granite City averaged nearly 47 points per game in the regional and sectional tournaments, that a high-scoring game should be expected.

Bozarth is quoted in the story as saying to his team at Tuesday's practice, "Now boys, this is going to be a light workout. We don't want any strenuous action, just enough to loosen up your muscles and keep you conscious of how to handle a ball.

"Relax everyone. Thursday night, when we take the floor against Streator, it's just another ball game."

It might have been "just another game" to Bozarth and his players, but the anonymous writer of the story wouldn't let the team forget about that blasted 1938 state tournament game.

"Besides having the great desire of any high school team in Illinois to win the state basketball title, Granite City will have another burning motive to do some fine playing in Champaign. Just two years ago, a Granite City team went to the state meet only to lose a first-round game.

"The Warriors want to show state tourney fans that Granite City had a tough break two years ago and Granite really has good basketball players."

One thing Bozarth didn't have to worry about in 1940 that he did in 1938 was the fact that his team played the final of eight first-round games, late Thursday night. The players in 1940 slept in their own beds the night before the Streator game, departing for Champaign-Urbana early Thursday morning, and were to arrive and check in to the Urbana Lincoln Hotel at around noon.

Perhaps with visions of 1938 still in his head, Bozarth decreed that first order for the team upon its arrival would be to take a nap and then perhaps watch some of the afternoon tournament action at George Huff Gymnasium on the campus of the University of Illinois.

"Folks in Granite City are right proud of this team representing it in the state meet," the Press-Record said. "Several hundred fans are already making plans to be in Champaign and cheer the Warriors. Then, too, every other fan of this territory will be on hand, cheering for the Warriors."

Of those "hundreds" of Granite City fans there was only one enthusiastic busload of black and red-clad Granite students who would make the 150-mile cross-state trip to Champaign. During the long trip the students composed a victory song, according to the student newspaper, the Granite High World.

"We came from Granite, we're here to win – it's a hundred to one, that we'll win," the song began. The students toured the University of Illinois campus, including, directly across the street from Huff Gym, the massive Armory, which for its time was considered an engineering marvel.

As for the Happy Warriors themselves, they showed up for their late Thursday night game, ready to transact business. Playing in front of a packed house at Huff Gym was a bit daunting, even for players like Phillip and Parsaghian, who had been there two years earlier.

"That was an awesome place for us to play," said Phillip, who would later go on to stardom in that same building. "I didn't even know where Champaign was before I went there.

"We played on a stage at our high school and there couldn't have been more than 1,000 seats in there. Huff held about 7,500 or 8,000. All of us were overwhelmed – until we started playing."

Granite City jumped out to a 13-2 lead to start the game. Streator came back, however, reeling off an 18-3 run, that must have sent a shudder of déjà vu up Bozarth's spine.

Streator actually grabbed a 20-16 lead in the second quarter, but this time the Warriors had plenty of energy in reserve. By halftime, Granite City had regained the lead at 26-23. Streator would never mount a serious challenge in the second half, as the

Warriors coasted to a relatively easy 45-31 victory. It would be their last "easy" game of the tournament.

Phillip led the way with 13 points, but had plenty of help from Parsaghian (12 points) and Gages (11 points). Finally, Phillip was being recognized for what he was, one of the greatest high school players ever to play in Illinois. And, just as suddenly, Granite City was being taken seriously as having a legitimate shot to win it all.

One report referred to Phillip as "a smooth piece of machinery and as cool as the proverbial cucumber. His basket shooting copped the fancy of the attendants."

Or as Daily Illini columnist Harpo Bloom wrote of Phillip: "Half the time he looks as if he doesn't know what's going on. You think he's awkward until you see him speed up his stride and feint with surprising quickness for a fellow who is just shade under 6 feet, 3 inches.

"Phillip takes his place alongside such men as Louis Boudreau and Herb Scheffler, when they played for Thornton and Springfield, respectively, as one of the outstanding men to appear in the history of the state tournament."

Phillip's incredible athletic gifts were the prime reason suddenly Granite City was considered a serious contender to win the three-day, 16-game extravaganza.

"How to explain the new greatness that Granite City took on to successfully survive the fast and favored contention that Streator, Dundee, Moline and Herrin offered is rather difficult," wrote sports writer

Elmer J. Hazzard in the Collinsville Herald. "Their chances were given only remote consideration, but after the 45-31 surprise they handed Streator, and the critics' and crowds' first look at Andy Phillip, the tourney sentiment began to swing somewhat toward the Bozarthmen."

18. PATIENCE IS A VIRTUE

As impressive as the red and black Men of Granite had been in disposing of Streator in the first round at Champaign, they still had much to prove.

The biggest question mark surrounding the team was whether or not it could deal with a team that played baseline-to-baseline basketball, a team that could used all 94 feet of the George Huff Gymnasium court to its advantage. Dundee was just such a team.

The Redbirds, who had won the state title as recently as 1938, were considered the chalk team of the tournament and the wave of the future for basketball. In recent years, teams like Springfield and Lou Boudreau's Thornton team had proved that speed and athleticism could be an integral part of successful basketball.

While Granite City, with its "slow-break" offense, was a throwback team, Dundee, which is located northwest of Chicago, was a team that could run and gun with the best of them. Additionally, Dundee had center John Schumacher a holdover from the 1938 state championship team, Ken Menke, who would later team up with Andy Phillip with the University of Illinois "Whiz Kids," and high-scoring Clarence Massier..

The Redbirds gave the crowds of Huff Gym a taste of what they were capable of doing when they blasted poor Rushville, 72-47 in their first-round game. They shot 31 of 84 (37%) from the floor that night, a good shooting percentage for that era, no doubt boosted by the fact that they were scoring so many layups off fast-break opportunities.

Dundee scored an amazing 27 points in the second period, an unheard total for those days, as it broke wide open its game with Rushville. For the contest, Massier scored 21 (8 of 20 shooting), Menke added 20 (9 of 16) and Schumacher added 8 (3 of 18).

Based on their history and their performance against Rushville, the courtside pundits were all but conceding the tournament to Dundee. Obviously, in what shaped up to be a classic battle of wills, Granite City had other ideas.

Although not a particularly tall team, the Warriors were a good rebounding team for three reasons: 1) Junior George Gages, at 6-foot, 3-inches, was a tenacious space eater in the middle and he was improving with every game. 2) Evon Parsaghian, although just 5-11, played four or five inches taller because of his leaping ability, and 3) Andy Phillip, who stood a shade under 6-3, was probably the best rebounder in the tournament because of his uncanny knack for sensing where rebounds would carom off to and crashing the boards from his guard position.

Granite City's ability to control the boards would be critical to stopping Dundee's fast-break offense which was predicated on its big men controlling the boards and outletting the ball to its speedy guards. Granite City's game plan was simple: Control tempo and control Dundee's fast break by denying rebounds and keeping one player (Hagopian) back to stop them from running.

The Warriors wasted no time imposing their will. But surprisingly, it wouldn't be Phillip who would lead Granite City in scoring on this day. Andy Hagopian, who was the team's third leading scorer for the season, but not known for his scoring, would be the surprising "go-to" guy on this day.

Hagopian scored the game's first points on a "long side shot" 45 seconds into the contest. Granite City jumped out to a 10-3 lead as all five starters scored in the first period. Phillip hit a pair of free throws, Parsaghian hit a one-hander, Gages scored on a rebound and Danny Eftimoff hit from the corner.

But Dundee was far from finished, netting three consecutive baskets to pull to within a point at, 10-9, through the first period. Massier gave Dundee its first lead on a corner shot early in the second period, but Gages hit 1 of 2 free throws to tie it at 11, midway through the period. That would be the first of nine times the game would be tied.

Hagopian and Massier were charged with double fouls and both players converted their free throw as the game remained tied at 12. Schumacher got loose on a fast break as Dundee regained the lead at 14-12, but free throws by Phillip and Parsaghian tied it again. Parsaghian gave Granite City a brief 16-14 lead but Schumacher's shot from the corner tied the game at the half, 16-16.

Eftimoff opened the second half scoring with his patented corner shot, but Massier knotted the game at 16 with a pair of converted free throws. Hagopian regained the lead for the Warriors with a free throw, but Schumacher gave Dundee an 18-17 lead with a one-handed corner shot.

With Dundee leading, 20-19, on a Menke basket late in the third quarter, the turning point of the game occurred. Massier committed his fourth and final personal foul, because in those days, four fouls resulted in game elimination.

He left the contest with one basket and just six points after having scored 21 points the night before against Rushville. Phillip converted the free throw, tying the score at 20.

Menke and Hagopian traded buckets, as did Phillip and Dundee's Richard Heidinger. Schumacher, a deadly shooter from the corner, hit again as Dundee surged ahead, 28-26, heading into the final period.

The fourth quarter was all Granite City. With Massier gone, the Redbirds were without a primary scoring option and it took its toll.

Gages scored in close to tie the game at 28, and Parsaghian's rebound basket put the Warriors ahead, for keeps, 30-28. Hagopian shook loose of his man Heidinger to scoot in for a layup and that built the lead to four.

Hagopian played the game of his lifetime against Dundee, leading the team with 10 points. A picture that ran in the Press-Record showed why. The lightning quick Hagopian was shown dribbling circles around the much-taller Heidinger.

"That was the best game of my career," Hagopian said. "They put a bigger player on me and I was able to get away from him a few times for baskets.

"I wasn't much of a scorer all season, but for some reason I was able to score more when the tournament started. It started in the regionals. I don't really know how to explain it, just gaining confidence and becoming more aggressive, I guess."

Menke scored what would turn out to be Dundee's only points of the fourth quarter on a layup, but Hagopian retaliated with a layup of his own on the other end to make it 34-30. Phillip's free throw with 45 seconds left ended the scoring at 35-30.

With the victory, the previously lightly-regarded Warriors had gone from being hunters to being the hunted.

"This outfit gave a world of promise in whipping Streator in the first round, and fulfilled every bit of that promise last night," wrote Harpo Bloom in the Daily Illini. "They have the height and although they rely mainly on a slow-breaking offense, can be fast when they choose."

Hagopian's 10 points weren't the only pleasant surprise for the Warriors on this day. All five starters scored at least two baskets with Phillip scoring eight points, Parsaghian adding seven, Gages six and

Eftimoff four. Ebbie Mueller, the only other Granite City player to enter the game, was held scoreless.

While it was a rare game in which Phillip didn't lead his team in scoring, he certainly led the team in other ways.

"Andy Phillip's great generalship, his rebounding and his floor play were the factors which took their toll," said one account of the game. "Phillip didn't score as heavily as in other games. He had too much work, directing the Warriors and his few shots just simply wouldn't go through the net."

The game boiled down to Granite City executing its game plan to perfection while Dundee strayed. After its 31 for 84 shooting exhibition against Rushville, Dundee was held to 13 of 54 shooting (24%) against the Warriors.

"We always felt that if a team pressed us and put pressure on us to pick up the pace, that it would give us some problems," said Phillip, recalling the Dundee game years later in a Press-Record story by Patrick Heston. "But none during the 1940 season ever did that ...not even Dundee.

"Dundee was a run-and-gun team, but for some reason they played our style right along with us that game. I don't know why. It's very strange. To this day, I don't understand it."

Apparently no one thought to ask Dundee coach Eugene DeLacey that question after the game. But DeLacey did offer strong praise for Granite City, as well as an ability to foresee the future.

"Those boys are fighters," said DeLacey of the Happy Warriors. "They work hard for what they get.

"And, when they are within reaching distance of that state title, they'll grab it and never let go."

Ironically, Phillip and Menke would later go on to be teammates on Illinois' great Whiz Kids teams and apparently the subject of this game was a sore spot with Menke for years.

"When I see him, he says he still can't believe we beat them," Phillip would say in later years.

19. OVERCOMING ADVERSITY

The victory over Dundee, the team favored to win it all, accomplished two things. It changed the perception of the Happy Warriors as a team just happy to be in Champaign to that of legitimate contender for the state title.

More importantly, however, it gave the team itself the confidence that going all the way was not just a wild dream. It was indeed doable.

"When we went over to Champaign, we had no idea what to expect," Hagopian said. "Winning a state championship wasn't even in our thoughts.

"But when we beat Dundee, we started to think about it. We figured if we could beat them, everybody was picking them to win it, then maybe we could beat anybody."

The Happy Warriors weren't the only ones thinking along those lines. Chalk it up to youthful exuberance and a dose of hyperbole, but Harpo Bloom, writing in the Daily Illini, the student newspaper of the University of Illinois, was thinking along those lines as well when he wrote:

"The Granite City-Dundee battle was the best game to be played thus far in the tournament and may have been the real state finals. Barring unforeseen circumstances, Granite City should be crowned the state champions tonight."

Now, if the Happy Warriors could just get Moline to cooperate. The Maroons, from the Quad Cities area of northwestern Illinois, showed no signs of being invincible in their first two state tournament games.

Moline struggled to beat a rather pedestrian Casey team, 28-23, in the first round. In Friday's quarterfinals, Moline pulled away late to trounce Lewisville, 49-32.

But appearances were perhaps a bit deceiving regarding the Maroons, who took a 20-5 record into their Saturday afternoon matinee semi-final contest with Granite City. While they weren't as tall as Streator nor nearly as quick as Dundee, they had good size, good speed and most importantly a balanced attack.

Moline wasn't a particularly high-scoring team, but every player on the team was capable of putting the basketball through the hoop. In their first two games combined, all five starters – led by Edsel Gustafson's 15 points – had scored at least 12 points.

Anyone expecting the Warriors to waltz into Saturday night's championship game without a battle, was soon brought back to reality. Moline pulled out to a 14-13 lead through the back-and-forth first period, but Granite City seemed to gain some traction early in the second period.

With Hagopian continuing to build on his new-found confidence and scoring prowess, the Warriors surged to a five-point lead, their largest of the game, early in the second period. But Moline rallied late in the half to apparently take charge at the break, 25-21.

Granite City scored the first four points of the third period to tie the game at 25, but again, Moline came back and regained the lead at 29-26 through three periods. Gustafson, Dave Brasmer, and Bob Johnson combined for five points as the Maroons outscored the Warriors, 5-1, in the opening minutes of the fourth quarter to grab a 34-27 lead. That would be the largest lead by either team in the contest and it made the outlook for Granite City bleak indeed.

It was at that point, with approximately seven minutes left in the game, when Andy Phillip took it upon himself to do something very uncharacteristic for himself, or for any player, for that matter. Without instructions from Bozarth, he called a timeout.

"It wasn't like Andy to chastise anyone or criticize anyone, even when we made mistakes," Hagopian said. "But he was a good leader and we listened to him.

"When he called that time out, he did it to try to get us back on track. His talk really pepped us up. Generally, his message was just for everybody to do their job and get things under control."

Apparently the thought of Phillip uncharacteristically calling for a timeout on his own, shocked the Warriors back on track. Phillip started the rally with a basket from the corner and George Gages scored inside to cut the Moline lead to a manageable three points.

Then, according to the Champaign News-Gazette report on the game, Phillip nailed a 35-footer with 2:15 left to make it a 34-33 game. Jack Turner made a free throw to build the Moline lead to 35-33, but Hagopian tied the game at 35 with a long shot with about two minutes remaining.

Bob Miller hit one of two free throws at the 1:45 mark to give Moline a 36-35 lead. On its next possession, Granite City had four shots close to the basket, but Phillip missed twice and Gages missed one. Finally, on the fourth try, Phillip tipped in Gages' miss to give Granite City a 37-36 lead.

Phillip hit a free throw with 1:10 left and Gages scored on a rebound with 35 seconds left as Granite City suddenly found itself leading, 40-36. Parsaghian converted a free throw and Brasmer hit a basket in the closing seconds as the Warriors nailed down the 41-38 victory to advance to the championship game, which would be played just four hours later.

Lost in all the excitement of the thrilling comeback was the fact that Hagopian was severely injured in the final minute of the contest. He collided with a Moline player in a scramble for a loose ball and suffered a separated shoulder.

"It was toward the end of the game and another guy and I went for a loose ball," Hagopian said. "I got the ball, but I separated my shoulder on the play.

"I left the game but by that time it was already decided. "I went into the locker room, took a shower and got dressed. Then they took me to the hospital. I had never been in a hospital before."

Hagopian was diagnosed to have a separated left shoulder and was warned by doctors not to play in the championship game that night against Herrin, a team that had earned its way into the finals by beating hometown favorites, Champaign, 21-17, in Saturday's first afternoon contest. Of course, he didn't listen.

He would make a token appearance against Herrin, but that's all it would be. Ironically, Hagopian had just come into his own as a scorer, averaging 10 points per game in the first three games in Champaign.

His 13 points against Moline were second only to Phillip's 16 points. Luckily for Granite City, Gages was still improving with every game and scored 10 points against the Maroons.

Parsaghian netted just two free throws against Moline and no one else on the team scored. Parsaghian and Danny Eftimoff were a combined 0 for 12 in field goal attempts against Moline.

"It was a mistake taking me to the hospital," Hagopian would later say. "It didn't do any good at all.

"It would have been better if I had spent time with the boys, been more active and mobile. It was painful, but by going to the hospital, that let it cool off.

"It's kind of ironic, but even after we came home, there was no attempt to ever get me to see a doctor. There are still things I can't do with my left shoulder. It's not as free as the right one."

20. A QUICK TURNAROUND

The problem with high school state basketball tournaments has always been the same. There are simply too many teams involved and too short a time span.

That was certainly the case in the 1940 Illinois High School Association state tournament. With a 16-team field involved, it was necessary to play eight games on Thursday and four more on Friday.

The reward for the four surviving teams was a doubleheader on Saturday. The luckiest team was the winner of Saturday's early game because that team, in this case Herrin, had a full six hours to rest up for that evening's championship game with its 8:15 p.m. tipoff.

The most unfortunate team was the loser of the late Saturday afternoon game. That team barely had time to wolf down and digest a hot dog before it was time to participate in that evening's 6:30 p.m. third-place game. There were probably teams over the years that didn't even bother to take showers or change clothes between games.

The next worst scenario was that of the winner of the second Saturday afternoon game. With the second game ending at approximately 4 p.m., that team had four hours to shower, change clothes, eat a light meal, rest and then prepare for the most important game of their lives.

Andy Hagopian doesn't remember what he had to eat that Saturday night of the most important game of his life, but he remembers it wasn't much.

"About all I remember is that at the hospital they put my left arm in a sling and that was about it," Hagopian said. "Leonard Davis came to get me and we got to Huff Gym around 6:30 or so, while the third place game was going on."

Hagopian's injury was apparently ligament damage to his left shoulder. While it wasn't deemed a "serious" injury it was extremely painful and he was unable to lift his left arm.

Hagopian explained that to Coach Bozarth when he arrived at Huff Gym, but Bozarth felt it was important that Hagopian be in the starting lineup that night against Herrin.

"I talked to Bozarth and told him that it was hurting, but he wanted me to play," Hagopian said. "It was a courtesy thing for me, he wanted me out there for the opening tipoff.

"But right after the first play he took me out. There was no way I could shoot the ball.

"I couldn't do anything. I would have done more harm than good on the floor."

The fact that Hagopian could not score presented a huge problem for Bozarth. Hagopian, just a junior, had been improving with every game and, like George Gages, had blossomed just in time for the state tournament.

While Parsaghian's scoring had declined over the course of the season, Hagopian and Gages had come on strong. Hagopian had averaged around six points per game for the entire season, but in the first three games in Champaign he had scored 30 points, an average of 10 per game, including a season-high 13 against Moline.

Bozarth knew that Hagopian would be limited so the player he designated to replace him was the seldom-used back-up guard Ed Hoff, who didn't score enough points during the season to register a meaningful scoring average. Hoff had seen only brief action in the Streator and Moline games and didn't play against Dundee.

Andy Phillip had his theory about why Bozarth thought it was so important that Hagopian be in the starting lineup that night. He recalled the situation in Patrick Heston's 1997 story in the Press-Record.

"Bozarth really wanted Hagopian to play, even though he was hurt and in a harness and everything," Phillip said. "Even if he couldn't shoot and score, Bozarth wanted him in there because he knew the plays so well. But it just couldn't be."

While the Warriors would be without Hagopian for the championship game, they would not be without support. On both sides of the tracks at home, support was gathering.

While, of course there was no television at that time and newspapers were unable to publish the results of the Saturday afternoon games before their Sunday papers would hit the streets with results of the evening games, there was a buzz in the streets of Granite City. Those who had radios in their homes, mostly those from east of the tracks, knew to have them tuned in for the game that night.

For those who didn't own their own radios, still a bit of a luxury item in Lincoln Place in those days, there would be a radio tuned to the game at the Lincoln Place Center "clubhouse" that night. Reports from that time say the game was translated into at least five languages as the championship game progressed that evening.

While the clubhouse provided more of a family atmosphere to listen to the game, it was reported that Sim's Place, a favorite haunt of the ethnics of Lincoln Place, was filled to capacity that night. Men of the neighborhood gathered at Sim's to imbibe in their favorite alcoholic beverage and shoot a game of pool.

The Granite City state tournament games were broadcast over a local station, WTMV. But apparently it took a last-ditch effort by the station to pick up the feed of the broadcast by frantically selling off advertising to local businessmen and individuals, who had never before advertised anywhere.

The town, especially in the Lincoln Place neighborhood, started to feel the excitement after the thrilling victory over Dundee on Friday night. Apparently there was plenty of loud fireworks and honking of horns when Granite City prevailed that night.

John Phillip was known to have made the trip over to Champaign that night to watch his son Andy play, but it is not known how many of the other parents made the trip.

"My parents had no idea what a big deal this was until afterwards," said Hagopian, whose parents listened to the game in Granite City. "They thought we were just playing more games.

"I had no idea myself what a huge deal it was, so how would they know? They would never see me play a game until the following season."

One of the Happy Warriors' biggest supporters was Ray "Hap" Duncan, a Granite City high school graduate who was a member of the football coaching staff and physical education department at the University of Illinois. Duncan, who had just authored a book entitled "Six-Man Football," was Granite City's unofficial tour guide the week of the tournament.

Duncan was happy to give tours of the campus, especially to the few Granite City students who were able to make the trek cross-state. He also helped the visitors find rooms in Champaign-Urbana, which at that time were very limited. On the night of the championship game, Duncan was said to have sneaked into the Happy Warriors' locker room and left a lucky penny on a bench where it was sure to be found.

Ebbie Mueller reportedly found the penny and showed it to his teammates, who all rubbed it for good luck.

Perhaps Granite City's most flamboyant fan that night was Elmer Hazzard, who doubled as a sports writer for the Collinsville newspaper. According to a report in the Press-Record, Hazzard "shouted, exhorted, applauded and gave advice to the team during the entire tournament.

"He collapsed from exhaustion following the Dundee game Friday night. He also suffered a bruised hand from pounding his fist, but recovered in time to see each game."

Apparently this was all before the "no cheering in the press box" rules were instituted.

21. TIME TO SHINE

"If the nations of Europe were as cooperative as you are, there would be no war. You are together, boys. Win." – a telegraph from Granite City High School Principal Paul Grigsby, to the Happy Warriors, on March 16, 1940.

Little did Grigsby know at the time how profound and meaningful his words would someday be. Granite City's own personal League of Nations, as one newspaper report would refer to the squad, would soon enough be personally involved in the goings on in Europe, but for tonight there was a basketball game to be played.

The opponent was Herrin, a team from deep southern Illinois, near Carbondale. While Bozarth didn't have an extensive scouting report on the Tigers, he didn't need one.

All he needed was to look into the mirror. The Tigers played the game the way Granite City liked it, slowly and deliberately.

Although it might not seem possible, Herrin was slower and more deliberate than Granite City was. The Tigers were at their offensive best in the first round and quarterfinal games, knocking off Chicago Heights Bloom, 30-25, and Paris, 29-22.

But in the semi-finals, Herrin played it close to the vest and ousted Champaign, 21-17. Herrin attempted jut 37 shots against Bloom, 41 against Paris and 32 against Champaign.

Even by 1940 standards, these were two very deliberate teams and this was going to be throwback basketball at its finest.

Apparently Bozarth wasn't a huge proponent of scouting reports, but the game plan for beating Herrin would be fairly simple. The Tigers passed the ball and ran their weave until they got exactly the shot they wanted.

When it was time to shoot, chances are the shooter would be either Fred Campbell, an all-state player who scored 28 points in Herrin's three previous tournament games, or Dallas Lillich, who netted 37 points over the same span. Both were proficient in the new-fangled one-handed shot, which at the time was still considered a "hot dog" shot in some corners of the state, including Granite City.

According to one report, the last thing the Happy Warriors did before taking the floor after Bozarth's pre-game speech, was to line up and honk the horn on "Little Betsy," which manager Harold Brown had positioned near the locker room's exit.

They took the floor for warm-ups before a Huff Gym full house crowd of 7,052. Attendance for the seven sessions of the tournament was 46,256, second highest in the tournament's history to that point in time.

"It was an incredible wonderful, once-in-a-lifetime experience," said Hagopian of taking the floor that night. "It was unforgettable."

The game did not start well for the Warriors. Just 15 seconds into the contest, Bozarth pulled the ailing Hagopian from the game in favor of Hoff. Campbell made the game's first basket as he took the opening tipoff, passed cross court to Lillich and scored a layup off the return pass. Lillich hit one of his patented one-handers from the left side and the Tigers were up 4-0.

Four minutes into the contest, Phillip put Granite City on the board with a long basket. But Campbell's second basket of the game made it 6-2. Phillip added a free throw, but Danny Eftimoff and Phillip followed with misses from the line. Finally Gages' rebound basket of a Phillip missed shot pulled the Warriors to within a point at 6-5.

But again, Campbell hit a one-hander that swished from the corner. Lillich got free under the basket to score and Herrin enjoyed a healthy 10-5 lead at the end of the first period.

Lillich, who was 17 of 26 from the free throw line in Herrin's four tournament games, expanded the Tigers' lead to 11-5 with a charity toss after being fouled by Eftimoff to open the second period. According to the Press-Record account of the contest, Granite City's inside game wasn't effective and they resorted to taking too many long shots at this point. At one point, according to the story, Granite City missed on three offensive putbacks in a row.

Evon Parsaghian made the second of two free throws after being fouled by Campbell to cut the lead to 11-6. Lillich responded with a 30-foot bank shot from the left side as Herrin led, 13-6.

Again, Parsaghian matched Lillich's bucket, hitting from the deep right corner, but Campbell broke loose for one of the rare fast break baskets of the game. Eftimoff fouled Campbell on the play, he made the free throw and Herrin enjoyed its largest lead of the game, 16-8.

"I can't remember exactly what happened at that point, but it wouldn't surprise me if Andy (Phillip) called one of his timeouts at that point to rally the team," said Hagopian.

Certainly, when the Happy Warriors trailed by eight points in such a low-scoring contest, it was the definite low point. Whatever Bozarth told his troops or whatever Phillip said to his teammates took hold.

Herrin wouldn't score again for the next 12 minutes. Unbelievably, Granite City's defense shut out Herrin's offense for the remainder of the first half, the full third period and the first few minutes of the fourth quarter.

Phillip scored the final three points of the first half as he got loose under the basket, scored off a Gages' assist and was fouled. Phillip made the free throw as Granite City cut the Herrin lead to 16-11 at the break.

For reasons only Bozarth can explain, he came back with Hagopian in the starting lineup to open the second half. As fate would have it, Granite City's sparkplug was fouled and sent to the free throw line almost immediately. As you might expect, he missed his free shot and returned to the bench in favor of Hoff.

"I didn't ask him to put me back out there, but it certainly hurt not being able to go into the game," Hagopian said.

Regarding his free throw attempt he said: "We shot our free throws underhand in those days and I can tell you, even that hurt very much. I came close, but missed it."

Neither team could generate much offense in the third period, but Herrin was absolutely stymied. Perhaps it was the reality that a state championship was minutes away from their grasp, but neither team played anywhere near their offensive capability in the third period.

By one account, Gages missed four putbacks and a free throw and was called for three seconds in the lane in the third period alone. Gages did manage to put in one rebound of a Phillip miss however. Phillip wasn't shooting particularly well himself, but his tip-in basket near the end of a third period that both teams would probably want to forget, brought the Warriors to within a point at 16-15.

Phillip was the man again as he maneuvered through the Herrin defense in transition to give Granite City its first lead of the contest, 17-16, to open the fourth quarter. But Herrin regained the lead at 18-17 as Edward Parsons scored his only points of the contest on a one-handed basket, as

Herrin broke its 12-minute drought with its first points of the second half.

Then Campbell rebounded a Gages' miss and dribbled to the free throw line where he nailed a basket that built the Herrin lead to 20-17. Phillip, sensing the urgency of the situation, drove all the way to the Herrin hoop, only to see his shot roll over the rim and out.

Parsaghian missed on the follow-up, but Phillip tipped in that rebound to make it 20-19. Campbell, perhaps sensing that the Happy Warriors' transition wasn't what it normally was with designated defender Hagopian on the bench, again went coast to coast to score. His layup put the Tigers ahead, 22-19, with four minutes to play.

Phillip, who at this point had taken over as Granite City's only scorer, was shoved going for a rebound of a Campbell miss by Junior Newlin. Phillip converted and the lead was 22-20.

Parsaghian, who was known to get tired late in games, might have been on his last legs when his man Parsons got loose from his defense and Parsaghian was forced to foul him. Parsons missed the free throw, but Bozarth, apparently upset with Parsaghian's defense or thinking he needed a rest, made the bold move of replacing his second leading scorer in the state title game with seldom used Ebbie Mueller.

It was a good substitution, however, as Parsaghian caught his breath and returned to the game seconds later at Herrin's time out with 52 seconds left. It got Parsaghian ready for what would be the most important minute and shot of his basketball career.

But first, however, the Warriors needed to tie the game at 22. That honor fell to Phillip, naturally, who with 36 seconds left, scored on an inbounds play under the Granite City basket, after a Herrin player had knocked the ball out of bounds. For Phillip, it was his ninth consecutive point and his 15th of Granite City's 22 points to that point.

"On a beautiful and bewildering out-of-bounds play, one sparkling with speed and clever, weaving ball-handling, Phillip eluded the entire Herrin defense to nail a set-up that tied the count at 22-22," wrote Hazzard. "The play became so fast and pressing that Granite City inadvertently committed a two-shot foul on Campbell."

A hush fell over the crowd when seconds later Phillip fouled Campbell, Herrin's best player and all-stater. It was Phillip's third foul and placed him one foul away from game elimination.

But Campbell missed both free throws and Phillip came down with the second miss. He passed ahead to Eftimoff, who dribbled deep into the Herrin defensive end and dished off to Hoff, who was only on the floor because of Hagopian's injury, near the free throw line.

Hoff may have been the last player on the floor Bozarth wanted handling the ball with the game on the line, but there he was driving to the hoop with 12 seconds lcft in the game.

Hoff, apparently unaware how many seconds were left on the clock and unable to find Phillip

– the player everyone in Huff Gym expected to take the final shot – panicked and began his drive to the hoop. Hoff slipped and fell in the lane and what seemed like the entire Herrin squad converged on him in an attempt to tie him up.

Miraculously, however, Hoff spotted Parsaghian – the forgotten man of the Granite City offense – darting to the basket, and from the seat of his pants, he rifled the perfect assist. Parsaghian, who had been just 1 of 8 from the floor in that game and 9 of 56 for the tournament, made the winning layup with about 8 seconds remaining. Accounts of the game have Parsaghian scoring the winning basket with 12 to four seconds remaining in the game.

"His nickname forever after that was 'Horizontal Hoff,'" Hagopian laughed. "That was his claim to fame."

According to one account, Hazzard, the excitable sports writer from Collinsville, "almost broke up the ball game himself in the final seconds of play. He dashed madly out on the floor, throwing his mauled green fedora in the air when Parsaghian scored the winning basket."

Campbell fouled Parsaghian on the basket with what one account described as a virtual "bear hug." The rules of the day at that time gave the aggrieved team the option of accepting the free throw opportunity or declining and retaining possession of the ball. That left Bozarth with an interesting dilemma.

Phillip, realizing that there was a viable option to Parsaghian shooting the free throw, signaled for a time out. Bozarth decided in the time out that the team would retain possession rather than shoot the free throw. For some reason, he decided seldom-used John Markarian would inbounds the ball to Phillip who would then dribble and heave the ball into the Huff Gym rafters as time expired.

But Herrin had other ideas. The Tigers forced a violation on the inbounds pass. The ball was inbounded to Campbell from under the Granite City basket and Campbell dribbled to halfcourt and let loose with a desperate heave that would have tied the game had it gone in. According to one game report the shot "bounded from the top of the backboard as the gun ended the game."

"We just held our breath until that last shot bounced away," Hagopian recalled.

22. PARTY TIME

Call it hyperbole, but the Granite City Press-Record account of the celebration that followed called it "the greatest display of enthusiasm that George Huff Gym has seen in its period of existence.

"Down from the stands swarmed the hilarious Granite City fans to affectionately pound the backs of the new state champs, raise them to their shoulders and attempt to carry them triumphantly to the locker room.

"Big dreamy Andy Phillip, the standout player of the tournament, finally broke into a grin as the tension of the past days lifted and realized Granite had finally attained its goal. He rested uncomfortably on a myriad of arms and rode a wave of acclaiming voices finally leaning across to shake the shaking hand of Evon Parsaghian, teammate who also was being tossed around by the friendly mob.

"The champs couldn't get away to the shower. First they had to talk over the radio, and then, when they finally did get downstairs, they had to trudge up again to receive that minor item, the trophy for which they have battled the past three weeks.

"Next to Phillip the crowd acclaimed Andy Hagopian, the boy who suffered a shoulder separation in the semi-final thriller with Moline and who played part of the second half to snap the Granite City club out of its lethargy at halftime."

Another post-game account painted a much different scene of the locker room after the team had finally received its trophy. "Champs are calm when it's over" claimed a headline in one scene-setter story after the game.

"Granite City's basketball team walked out of its dressing quarters at 8:15 Saturday night, just a state finalist; about an hour later it walkcd in as a state champion and there was little difference." began a story written by T.O. White.

"Winning a state title and coming to the realization of the fact seems to be two different things. At any rate the boys were just as calm after the game as they had been several times during the tournament when calm and care were the price of victory."

The story painted a humorous picture of Hagopian, a bit bemused by the situation.

"Andy Hagopian had a little more difficult time of it than any of his mates. He wanted to accept the handshakes and congratulations, but his shoulder was giving him plenty of pain, which he had laughed off during the basketball game.

"He could not even smile when Spike Dixon removed the tape and bandage which had been necessary to protect the injury.

"Andy Hagopian was almost ready for the shower before he said a word. 'The state champions,' he said quietly to nobody in particular. 'Can you imagine that?'"

Also seen in the Huff Gym's expansive basement locker room, Andy Phillip was receiving a hearty hug from his father John, one of the few Granite City parents to make the trip to Champaign. According to the account, the elder Phillip "was much more excited than the boys."

Phillip would receive an even more tangible reward. University of Illinois basketball coach Doug Mills (1936-47), an interested observer in Huff Gym all week, would call Phillip the best all-around prep player he had seen in eight years and according to legend offered Phillip a basketball scholarship on the spot.

"Evon Parsaghian and George Gages hugged each other twice, and Dan Eftimoff and Ed Mueller shook hands. All of the room was noisy, but the boys were not responsible.

"Ray Duncan, a Granite City boy, was more excited than the players, as was Ab Duncan, a great booster for the Southwestern Conference."

As for Coach Bozarth, he was whisked away immediately after the game for a radio interview.

"Was (Bozarth) excited?" the account asked rhetorically. "Well somebody said he was seen kissing somebody else's wife. The excuse was he was so elated over winning the state tournament that he did not know what he was doing."

Bozarth's remarks on the radio are lost forever, but he did have a precious few comments for the press immediately after the game. As always, Bozarth was gracious and humble.

"Coach Byron Bozarth said that the greatest thing about the entire tournament was the friendship, sportsmanship, fellowship and the decency of all the coaches and teams at the tourney and the fine treatment they received from the University authorities. Pop Dale of Streator, Eugene Delacy of Dundee, George Seneff of Moline and Russell Emery of Herrin, coaches of the teams that Granite City defeated, were particularly fine in their attitude toward the team that defeated them in the games."

If the Happy Warriors were subdued in the locker room, they weren't when they got back to their hotel rooms that night.

"We had curfews all week, but not that night," Hagopian said. "We had our friends come over to our rooms and we stayed up all night laughing and talking.

"We were too excited to sleep."

If their eyes weren't too tired to focus the next morning, the Happy Warriors would have read this fine account of their achievement in Sunday's edition of the Champaign News-Gazette:

"There is joy tonight in Granite City. Joy around the Vartan Market and the beauty parlor of Eftimoff. Joy down where Kirchoff's Grocery lies hard by Mitseff's Market with Stoyanoff's Dry Goods not far away.

"For Granite City won the state high school basketball championship. It beat Herrin here tonight, 24 to 22, to become the last of the 898 in the survival of the fittest, the first southern champion in 11 years and the first regional runnerup in history to win the title. Evon Parsaghian's basket with 12 seconds to play gave Granite City the victory.

"Attendance for the final game was 7,052 and for the seven sessions of the classic, 46,256. Total attendance was second highest in history.

"They fight to the Last"

"Fighting sons of the Armenian, Bulgarian, German, Yugoslav and Magyar came back to whip Herrin in the fashion so typical of their four state tournament victories. In every game except one, they were behind when the last period started. But these boys are fighters and sons of fighters. Most of their parents came over from Europe after the last World War and they've battled their way up.

"Granite City is one of the greatest fourth quarter clubs ever to step onto the floor of Huff Gym. The Warriors trailed Dundee 28-26 going into the last period and they won 35-30. They were 29-26 behind Moline and then pulled that game out of the fire, 41-38. Herrin had them 16-15 and lost 24-22. Granite City outscored every one of its four opponents in both the third and fourth quarters. No team had the second half drive which Granite City possessed."

In one of his last interviews in 1997, Phillip said this about winning the championship to the Press-Record.

"I look back and I don't know how we did it," Phillip said. "We were just a bunch of kids. We had no idea what we were doing or what it would mean in the future.

"We were just a bunch of kids, coming together as a true melting pot, playing basketball and having a real good time in the process. That's all."

23. IT WILL NEVER BE THE SAME

The Granite City that the Happy Warriors returned to early Sunday afternoon looked in every way to be the same place the team had left three days earlier.

Physically, it was the same. Granite City High School, the YMCA and the downtown were still on the east side of the railroad tracks. The steel mills and Lincoln Place were still to the west of the tracks.

But the heart and soul of the "Pittsburgh of the West" changed forever at around 9:30 p.m., March 16, 1940. It was at that time that a small cadre of teen-aged boys from a 10-square block ghetto put Granite City on the map of Illinois.

It would take World War II to make things better for the few black men and their families, who worked in Granite City's steel mills. After fighting in the battlefields of Europe and Pacific, they would no longer have to heed the 9 p.m. factory whistle to evacuate the city where they worked.

But for Granite City's white subclass, the immigrants of Lincoln Place, the changes were immediate and stunning.

"It changed everything," said Andy Hagopian, who in his senior year would be elected president of the Granite City student body. "For one thing, (him being elected student body president) never would have happened if I hadn't played on a state championship basketball team.

"But that made us accepted in Granite City, in a way I never felt accepted before. Where we lived in Lincoln Place could best be described as a ghetto. All our parents were working in the mills, nobody had any wealth. We were just very ordinary people.

"But after that, people from the other side of the tracks started to come down there. They knew it was okay to come to Lincoln Place after that.

"After we won the state championship, we were no longer viewed as the kids from the wrong side of the tracks. We were accepted.

"Suddenly we had opportunities. People didn't seem to care about the tracks anymore."

Andy Phillip, when interviewed for Patrick Heston's 1997 story in the Granite City Press-Record, agreed with Hagopian.

"It kind of helped Lincoln Place be accepted as part of the city and not just as that place beyond the tracks," said Phillip, who months later would be departing for the University of Illinois, never again to return to Granite City as a full-time resident.

What the Granite City basketball team did find waiting for them when they returned that Sunday was an adoring crowd, actually two adoring crowds. The team's first stop was at the high school and that was followed by a trip to Lincoln Place.

"There was a big crowd waiting for us at the high school, and then we all went down to Lincoln Place," Hagopian recalled. "There was even a bigger crowd down there.

"There was nothing planned, just a huge celebration. There was whooping and hollering and firecrackers. I don't know if we realized what we had done till we saw all the people turn out."

Granite City Mayor M.E. Kirkpatrick delivered a speech of welcome at the high school and Coach Bozarth introduced his players. From there, an impromptu parade formed, led by boys and girls on bicycles, followed by the school band, the team bus and a caravan of automobiles.

According to one report, the parade, which included motorcycles "popping in and out," stretched for over a mile. All the way to Lincoln Place, the sidewalks were lined with smiling, waving admirers.

The parade made an impromptu stop near Sim's Place when the crowd swarmed the team bus, chanting, "We want our boys, we want our boys!" Sim's proprietor Sim Bagosian gave away $72 in firecrackers, according to one report, although there was a city ordinance in place banning the noisemakers.

The crowd near Sim's made it impossible for the bus to pass, so the team disembarked and walked the final block and a half to the place where it all began – Sophia Prather's Lincoln Place Community Center. To get there, the crowd had to pass by Queenie Elieff's beauty parlor, where the Warriors' Regional and Sectional championship trophies were already on display. An outdated sign in Queenie's window said "Let's get the rest of them," and when the celebration ended, the trophy symbolizing the state championship also ended up in Queenie's window, albeit temporarily.

"We won for Granite City and for Lincoln Place," captain Andy Phillip told the cheering crowd.

A hastily lettered banner across the street from the gathering said "Welcome State Champions." Another sign, hoisted by Lincoln Place merchant John Varadian just said "welcome home" and the sign ended up tacked to a tree in front of Phillip's home at 1610 Maple Street.

"Emotional people, these residents of Lincoln Place," said another account of the celebration. "Tears were shed. Firecrackers were popping. It was a great day for Lincoln Place. Sophia Prather was with her people again."

Miss Prather, a battler for the people of Lincoln Place, certainly would have been proud of her boys, but she would have been proud of the changes that would soon sweep the city as well. Dick King, Granite City High School's president in 1939, who went on to become a Broadway actor, claims his native city's prejudice was founded more in snobbery than it was mean-spiritedness.

"What those boys did for Granite City is outstanding," King said. "There is still prejudice in Granite, just like there is everywhere else in America, but at least it's not as blatant as it once was. And, the incredible thing is it happened overnight.

"When they won the state tournament, they broke down the boundary of prejudice against the people of Lincoln Place. They could have all been elected mayor if they had wanted to...that's how popular they were.

"They broke down the barriers engrained in all of us. I always thought all the kids from Lincoln Place were all "Honkies" or Hungarians. It turns out Andy (Phillip) is the only Hungarian in the group, but it didn't make any difference any more.

"If anything, it was a snobbery more than anything else. Granite City is a very friendly town, so it's kind of a paradox. But there was this engrained feeling that there was a difference between races and the ethnic groups."

Helen Gages, the widow of George Gages, grew up on the so-called "right side" of Granite City's railroad tracks, so she has a unique perspective of the city's transformation.

"We were downtown people and they weren't," she said. "When George and his team won the state basketball title, though, that changed things here.

"People realized they weren't any different than anybody else. I don't know how bad it was for them, but I know it was different. When you crossed the tracks, you knew you were in a different place."

For Hagopian, Markarian and the rest of the Lincoln Place group, there were tangible and immediate changes.

"All of a sudden, everybody knew us and we were everybody's friend," Hagopian said. "We were invited to all the parties and participated in events that we never would have been welcomed at before."

Added Markarian: "We felt more accepted by everyone in the town. That included the girls and we'll leave it at that."

A tidbit in the Press-Record summed things up this way: "Nothing is too good for these boys." There was talk of beginning a fund to buy the entire team wrist watches but it was discovered that that would be a violation of IHSA rules, so the plan was dropped.

"We never got the watches but the thought was there," Hagopian said. "It was against the rules."

There were no rules against dinners and banquets, however, and the team was feted at at least a dozen affairs in the months that followed. Among the dinners on their busy schedule were banquets at the Presbyterian Men's Club, the Optimist Club, The Elks Club the Southwestern Illinois Conference banquet and various dinners at individual homes.

"We ate like kings," Hagopian recalled. "Everybody loved us."

Another account of the celebration, written by T.O. White of the Champaign News-Gazette, seemed to hint at big changes in store for Granite City.

"You folks who saw Granite City play, know that there is no differences among the players, and there is really no differences between the mother city and the foreign settlement," White wrote, alluding to Lincoln Place. "However, there is a big racial separation and the background of those in Lincoln Place are for the most part quite in contrast to those out of it.

"Seven of the ten boys on the squad are first generation Americans and the parents are glad not only for their boys' success but for the fact that the children are being brought up in a country where success is not predicated upon race or creed or color. So they naturally displayed more emotion, since the winning of the state championship was a visible indication that their boys were so good and even better than any other five boys the state could boast."

24. EPILOGUE

Isabel Vartan will never forget the hot summer day in 1945 when she drove to St. Louis' Union Station to pick up her brother, Evon Parsaghian, who was taking a "rest and relaxation" visit from the carnage he had witnessed first-hand as a U.S. Marine in the South Pacific.

Parsaghian had enlisted in the Marines shortly after World War II had broken out in December of 1941, and he jumped right into the meat grinder that was the South Pacific. Like his high school teammate Andy Phillip, Parsaghian saw action and plenty of it. While Phillip fought in the bloody battle of Iwo Jima, Parsaghian fought in the fierce battle for Tarawa, Nov. 20-23, 1943.

"Evon was in seven major battles in the South Pacific," Isabel, his younger sister, said proudly of her big brother. "It had a big effect on him."

Isabel noticed that effect the day she went to pick up her brother in St. Louis. Parsaghian had just received word that the ship he had been assigned to, the U.S.S. Indianapolis, had been sunk.

The Cruiser, commissioned in 1932, survived Pearl Harbor and was able to deliver the atomic bomb dropped on Hiroshima to the Philipines for assembly, but it couldn't survive an attack by a Japanese submarine on its return trip on July 30, 1945. It was just weeks before war would end.

Only 316 crew members, roughly one quarter of the 1,199 men on board at the time, would survive as the Indianapolis sunk to the bottom of the South Pacific Ocean 12 minutes after it was hit.

The news, as you would expect, hit Parsaghian hard, but at that time he had no idea of the true terror that was in store for his shipmates. About 900 of the crew members survived their ship's sinking, but approximately two thirds of the survivors fell victim to the worst shark attack on humans in recorded history.

The plight of the Indianapolis was well chronicled in the movie "Jaws" by the Robert Shaw character. The Indianapolis' captain, Charles McVeigh. was court-martialed in 1968 for not maneuvering the Indianapolis in a serpentine manner to avoid a torpedo attack, but he was later exonerated in 1999.

When he disembarked from the train that day in St. Louis, Parsaghian and his fellow Marine traveling companion had been drinking heavily. The binge was precipitated by the news of the Indianapolis.

"I remember Evon and his buddy, they were talking about all their buddies on the Indianapolis, guys named Joe and Arthur," Isabel said. "They were totally drunk.

"All their friends had gone down with the Indianapolis and they were drinking to their memory.

He told me he didn't want to come home with me because he didn't want our parents to seem him like that. He told me to come back and pick him up the next day.

"I was amazed to see my brother like that. He never took a drink until he enlisted in the Marines. He was just a kid when he enlisted – 18 years old. When he came home he had pictures from some of the battles, dead bodies everywhere. It was so gruesome.

"Evon lost a lot of friends and he had a hard time with that. I don't think he ever got over all of it. He saw an awful lot over there. It was very traumatic for him."

Parsaghian cheated death on numerous occasions during the war, but his experiences took a toll on him. He attended the University of Illinois briefly but returned to the Metro East area to work at a sheet metal plant in Alton, Ill, while continuing to play semi-professional basketball.

Parsaghian held numerous jobs over the years including reenlisting in the Marine Corps., where he served as a Staff Sergeant for years and later working for the state of Illinois. He passed away in 1988, while working at a dairy in Fort Myers, Fla.

Like Parsaghian, Andy Phillip served in the Marines in the South Pacific during World War II. After leaving the University of Illinois midway through his illustrious career there, he enlisted in the Marines and saw fierce action at Iwo Jima as a forward artillery observer.

Phillip, who attained the rank of first lieutenant, was on the island for the entire 25 days it was needed to subdue the Japanese forces dug into the lava rock. The bloody battle cost 6,800 American lives but Phillip survived without a scratch.

"I slept in pill boxes with burned bodies," Phillip told legendary sports writer Murray Olderman.

His basketball career was well-documented. He enjoys membership in the Naismith Basketball Hall of Fame, inducted in 1961, as well as the State of Illinois Hall of Fame and the Granite City Hall of Fame. He is the only player from the University of Illinois ever inducted into the Naismith Hall.

Phillip went on to coach two professional teams, the St. Louis Hawks of the NBA and the Chicago Stags of the ABL after his 11-year NBA career ended in 1958. Additionally, Phillip gave professional baseball a whirl, pitching and playing first base for the St. Louis Cardinals' Class AAA Columbus Cardinals from 1947 through 1951.

Tragedy visited Phillip twice later in life. His first wife, Dorothy, whom he met while she was skating in Sonja Henie's Ice Show, died at a young age of cancer. Their son Steve, a football star at Palm Springs (Calif.) High School, died of cirrhosis of the liver at age 52.

Phillip met his second wife Corky while visiting Granite City for a reunion of the basketball team in 1980. After leaving coaching, Phillip held numerous jobs, including running his own restaurant in Palm Springs that he called Andy Phillip's Hoop.

He also sold cars, was a substitute teacher and a basketball referee. For 24 years he was a juvenile probation officer for Riverside County, retiring in 1987. He passed away April 28, 2001 at the age of 78.

Danny Eftimoff also interrupted his education at the University of Illinois to enlist in the U.S. Army as an anti-aircraft operator in the South Pacific. When he returned from the war, he moved to Summit, Ill., to work in a restaurant owned by his sister and brother-in-law, Vera and Nick Gitcho.

When the restaurant closed a few years later, Eftimoff got into the construction business, first as a carpenter, then later as a contractor and eventually as a developer. He owned his own company, Danny's Builders.

Eftimoff married Irene Pishos of Summit, and they had two children, Danny and Christine. Eftimoff passed away, June 4, 2001 at the age of 79.

George Gages, who began the 1940 season playing behind Everett Daniels, developed into such a strong post player that he was offered a scholarship to play basketball at Bradley University after his graduation from Granite City High School.

"He had to turn it down," said his wife, Helen. "He was the sole supporter of his family so he had to go to work."

He didn't work long, however, as war broke out and he joined the U.S. Navy. Gages served on board the destroyer, the U.S.S. Twinning during the war.

He returned to Granite City and worked for 39 years at McDonnell Douglas Aircraft in St. Louis. The

Gages had one son, Allen, who died in an automobile accident in 1986 at the age of 29.

Gages passed away in the spring of 2006.

Like the other four starters on the 1940 squad, Andy Hagopian saw plenty of action during World War II. Originally drafted into the U.S. Army, Hagopian requested and was granted a transfer to the U.S. Air Force, where he entered the cadet program.

He reached the rank of Second Lieutenant and served as bombardier in Europe. Based in Italy in the latter stages of the conflict, he flew 21 missions over Germany.

He started his college career at Southern Illinois University, but later transferred to the University of Illinois, where he received a B.S. in marketing and accounting in 1949.

He owned several dry cleaning businesses in the St. Louis area until retiring in 1985. He is still very active in St. Gregory's Armenian Apostolic Church of Granite City, where he has served as parish president.

Hagopian's first wife, Angeline, who gave him three sons – Michael, Steven and Jeffrey – passed at an early age. He married his second wife Annette in 1974 and the couple still lives in Granite City.

Ed Hoff was a long-time supervisor with the Army Corps of Engineers and lived most of his life in Granite City where he and his wife Cathryn had three sons. He retired at 55 and moved to Naples, Fla. where he died in 2004.

Ebbie Mueller was a district sales representative for General Motors, representing Oldsmobile for the

Chicago area. He graduated from the University of Illinois, married a former Miss Illinois contestant and had two children.

Markarian, like Hagopian, remains in Granite City, as the only two known survivors from the squad. He is retired from McDonnell Douglas Aircraft in St. Louis, where he was a supervisor for 38 years, retiring in 1986.

Markarian's wife Anna died in auto accident in 1993. He has four children, John, Ronald, Randall and Cynthia, and all three boys are in the dental field.

Sam Mouradian served in the U.S. Army during World War II, then moved to the Los Angeles area and little is known about what became of him. Everett Daniels lived in Wood River for years, but shunned any efforts to be a part of team functions in the years that passed.

Team manager Harold Brown, whose "Little Betsy" contraption remains one of the quaint stories of Illinois high school folklore, was Granite City's park's director from 1959 through 1982. At that time, he retired to Ocala, Fla., where he still resides.

Leonard Davis, Bozarth's popular young assistant coach, eventually got out of teaching and coaching and served as Granite City's mayor for years. His widow Hulda, who with Bozarth's wife "Shep" wrote the Granite City High School song, still lives in Granite City.

Bozarth coached one more season after his championship, temporarily quitting teaching and coaching after the 1941 school year and a disappointing 9-19 season. Hagopian and Gages were the only returning starters from the 1940 championship team and both graduated in January at mid-term, a common practice in those days.

"It just wasn't the same the next year," Hagopian said. "We just weren't that good."

Bozarth accepted a lower paying job as civilian athletic counselor at Chanute Air Force Base in Rantoul, Ill., near Champaign. Bozarth left Granite City six months before the outbreak of World War II, but he did it because he "saw a need in all the boys away from home at Chanute.'

"At Granite City High School, I can be in contact with some 700 or 800 boys," Bozarth told the Champaign News-Gazette at the time. "At Chanute Field, I can touch 17,000 boys."

Bozarth returned to Granite City in 1947 and coached basketball and football for six more seasons before retiring from teaching in 1952. But he would never have another winning season in basketball and just one winning season in football in his second stint at the school.

Bozarth finished his career as an instructor at Miami (of Ohio) University. He passed away in 1975.

Bozarth later would call winning the state championship in 1940 the "realization of a lifetime's dream."

"I will keep trying for another title," he said, upon returning for his second stint at Granite City. "But if I never win again, I will always cherish those days as my most fond memories."

The Happy Warriors

47	Andy Phillip, capt.	G Sr.
44	Andy Hagopian	G Jr.
42	George Gages	C Jr.
50	Evon Parsaghian	F Sr.
43	Dan Eftimoff	F Sr.
41	Ebbie Mueller	F Sr.
49	Everett Daniels	C Jr.
45	John Markarian	F Jr.
46	Sam Mouradian	F Fr.
38	Ed Hoff	G Sr.

Byron Bozarth	Coach
Leonard Davis	Asst. Coach
Harold Brown	Manager
Paul A. Grigsby	Principal

Granite City's championship season

1939-40

29-5

1939

Dec. 5	Staunton (H)	W	38-23
Dec. 9	Livingston (A)	L	25-15
Dec. 15	East St. Louis (H)	W	36-20
Dec. 16	Livingston (H)	W	31-29
Dec. 19	Benld (A)	W	42-30
Dec. 22	Wood River (A)	L	20-19

Granite City's championship season

Mount Vernon Tournament

Dec. 27	Mattoon (first round)	W	45-39
Dec. 28	Quincy (quarter-finals)	W	41-17
Dec. 29	West Frankfort (semi-finals)	W	45-22
Dec. 30	Salem (championship game)	W	32-29

1940

Jan. 5	Madison (A)	W	49-20
Jan. 6	Collinsville (H)	W	37-31
Jan. 12	Edwardsville (A)	W	35-23
Jan. 13	Belleville (H)	W	27-22
Jan. 19	Alton (A)	W	45-26
Jan. 26	East St. Louis (A)	W	33-20
Jan. 30	Madison (H)	W	40-23
Feb. 2	Wood River (H)	W	19-17
Feb. 9	Collinsville (A)	L	41-28
Feb. 10	Edwardsville (H)	W	49-20
Feb. 16	Belleville (A)	W	42-21
Feb. 17	Mount Vernon (H)	W	33-30
Feb. 20	Gillespie (H)	L	41-39
Feb. 23	Alton (H)	W	61-30

IHSA Regional at Edwardsville

Feb. 29	Madison	W	64-22
March 1	Edwardsville	W	57-26
March 2	Wood River	L	32-28

IHSA Sectional at Highland

March 6	Jerseyville	W	64-27
March 7	Livingston	W	32-16
March 8	Wood River	W	36-22

Granite City's championship season

IHSA State Finals at Champaign-Urbana

March 14	Streator (first-round)	W	45-31
March 15	Dundee (quarter-final)	W	35-30
March 16	Moline (semi-final)	W	41-38
March 16	Herrin (final)	W	24-22

Southwestern Illinois Conference standings

1939-40 season

Granite City	12-2
Wood River	12-2
Collinsville	10-4
Edwardsville	9-5
Alton	5-9
Belleville	4-10
East St. Louis	4-10
Madison	0-14

Byron Bozarth's coaching records

Basketball

1927-28	8-10
1928-29	15-7
1929-30	19-4
1930-31	NA
1931-32	NA
1932-33	NA

Byron Bozarth's coaching records

Basketball

1933-34	19-4
1934-35	26-4
1935-36	13-13
1936-37	12-16
1937-38	25-7
1938-39	18-10
1939-40	29-5
1940-41	9-19
1947-48	8-14
1948-49	12-12
1949-50	11-16
1950-51	5-20
1951-52	10-18
1952-53	3-21

Football

1927	6-3-1
1928	9-0*
1929	3-5-2
1930	8-0-2*
1931	5-4
1932	6-2-1*
1933	2-7
1934	3-6-1
1935	1-8-1
1936	8-1*
1937	6-3-1
1938	7-2-1
1939	2-6-1
1940	4-4

Byron Bozarth's coaching records

Football
1947	4-5
1948	5-5
1949	4-4-2
1950	6-4
1951	4-6
1952	1-8
Totals	94-83-12

*Southwestern Illinois Conference champions

Leonard Davis' basketball coaching records

1941-42	12-13

Approximate scoring averages 1940

	Pts.	Games	Ave.
Danny Eftimoff	28	19	1.75
Ebbie Mueller	27	16	1.68
Evon Parsaghian	175	20	8.75
Everett Daniels	38	16	2.3
Andy Phillip	276	20	13.8
Andy Hagopian	124	20	6.2
George Gages	89	18	4.9

1940 Illinois State Basketball finals

First Round

Champaign (H.S.) 44	Chicago (Crane) 25
Salem 55	Beardstown 29
Herrin (H.S.) 30	Chicago Heights (Bloom Twp.) 25
Paris 36	Taylorville 35 (OT)
Moline (H.S.) 28	Casey 23
Lewistown 31	Hebron 30
Dundee 72	Rushville 47
Granite City 45	Streator (Twp.) 31

Quarterfinals

Champaign (H.S.) 34	Salem 30
Herrin (H.S.) 29	Paris 22
Moline (H.S.) 49	Lewistown 32
Granite City 35	Dundee 30

Semifinals

Herrin (H.S.) 21	Champaign (H.S.) 17
Granite City 41	Moline (H.S.) 38

Third Place

Moline (H.S.) 51	Champaign (H.S.) 33

Final

Granite City 24	Herrin (H.S.) 22

Summary of State Finalists

	School	Coach	W-L	Enroll
1	Granite City	Byron Bozarth	29-5	1580
2	Herrin (H.S.)	Russell Emery	23-8	900
3	Moline (H.S.)	Roger Potter	21-6	1176
4	Champaign (H.S.)	Harry Combes	26-8	996
	Dundee	Eugene DeLacey	25-3	448
	Lewistown	George Dertinger	27-5	355
	Paris	Ernie Eveland	31-6	716
	Salem	Mike Lenich	29-6	664
	Beardstown	L.M. "Nick" Carter	26-7	550
	Casey	Glen Rose	20-9	320
	Chicago (Crane)	Samuel Edelcup	16-4	5832
	Chicago Heights (Bloom Twp.)	Cecil Sarff	20-3	1836
	Hebron	A.E. Willett	30-2	101
	Rushville	Robert Wixom	26-7	332
	Streator (Twp.)	Lowell "Pops" Dale	22-9	1150
	Taylorville	Dolph Stanley	21-11	694

Top Scorers and Scoring Totals of All Teams

Player	School	G	FG	FT	Pts
Andy Phillip	Granite City	4	19	15	53
Dallas Lillich	Herrin (H.S.)	4	14	16	44
Fred Campbell	Herrin (H.S.)	4	16	9	41
Bob Johnson	Moline (H.S.)	4	15	6	36
Ken Menke	Dundee	2	15	3	33
Dave Brasmer	Moline (H.S.)	4	15	3	33
Sidney McAllister	Champaign (H.S.)	4	13	4	30

Top Scorers and Scoring Totals of All Teams

Player	School	G	FG	FT	Pts
Andy Hagopian	Granite City	4	13	4	30
George Gages	Granite City	4	13	4	30
Clarence Massier	Dundee	2	9	8	26
Evon Parsaghian	Granite City	4	10	6	26
John Tarrant	Champaign (H.S.)	4	13	0	26
Jack Turner	Moline (H.S.)	4	9	8	26

UPI All-Tournament Team

Player	School
Fred Campbell (F)	Herrin
George Gages (C)	Granite City
Dallas Lillich (G)	Herrin
Ken Menke (F)	Dundee
Andy Phillip (G)	Granite City

Second team

Andy Hagopian	Granite City
David Brasmer	Moline
Edsel Gustafson	Moline
Elton Meredith	Salem
Floyd Wilson	Paris

AP All-Tournament team

Player	School
Andy Phillip (G)	Granite City
Ray Grierson (G)	Champaign
Edsel Gustafson (C)	Moline
Fred Campbell (F)	Herrin
John Schumacher (F)	Dundee

Second team

Evon Parsaghian (F)	Granite City
Andrew Hagopian (G)	Granite City
Dick Gray (F)	Salem
Don McVey (C)	Champaign
Dallas Lillich (G)	Herrin

1940 All-State team

Player	School
Andy Phillip (G)	Granite City
Eugene Vance (G)	Clinton
Ed Parker (C)	Morton (Cicero)
Dwight Eddleman (F)	Centralia
Kenneth Menke (F)	Dundee

Second team

John Semanek (F)	Livingston
Fred Campbell (F)	Herrin
Laverne Hahs (C)	Bradley
George Jent (G)	Johnson City
Joe Astroth (G)	Wood River

Player of the year: Phillip

Champaign (H.S.) 44, Chicago (Crane) 25

First Round Game at Champaign [UI, Huff Gym]
Thursday, March 14, 1940

CHAMPAIGN (H.S.)

Player	FG	FGA	FT	FTA	Pts	PF
Amos Dickey	0	0	0	0	0	0
Maurice Dolan	2	5	1	3	5	1
Ray Grierson	3	12	1	3	7	4
Noel Hannah	0	1	1	1	1	0
Sidney McAllister	4	9	0	1	8	2
Don McVey	0	4	2	5	2	3
Jack Moore	0	4	0	1	0	3
John Tarrant	8	14	0	1	16	1
Bill Tull	1	3	0	0	2	2
Dean Woody	1	4	1	2	3	1
TOTAL	**19**	**56**	**6**	**17**	**44**	**17**

CHICAGO (CRANE)

Player	FG	FGA	FT	FTA	Pts	PF
Bernard "Buddy" Burro	0	4	0	0	0	4
Walter Dobranski	0	0	0	0	0	0
Ben Erkes	1	5	0	2	2	1
Bernie Goldberg	5	21	5	7	15	3
William Matters	0	0	0	0	0	0
Bernard Shapiro	0	1	0	1	0	0
Frank Stoikovich	0	1	0	0	0	2
Abraham Troop	0	0	0	0	0	0
Roman Wieszczyk	0	4	1	4	1	3
Ed Zuber	3	18	1	3	7	1
TOTAL	**9**	**54**	**7**	**17**	**25**	**14**

Champaign (H.S.)	15	9	(24)	10	10	(20)	–44
Chicago (Crane)	6	5	(11)	9	5	(14)	–25

Salem 55, Beardstown 29

First Round Game at Champaign [UI, Huff Gym]
Thursday, March 14, 1940

SALEM

Player	FG	FGA	FT	FTA	Pts	PF
Gerald Brubaker	4	5	2	3	10	3
Bill Finks	3	12	1	1	7	4
Dick Gray	4	14	2	3	10	4
Henry Hinckley	0	1	0	1	0	0
Max McGraw	0	2	0	0	0	0
James Meador	2	3	1	3	5	2
Elton Meredith	7	22	3	3	17	2
Daryl Robb	2	9	2	2	6	3
Bob Scoles	0	0	0	0	0	0
Jim Somer	0	1	0	0	0	0
TOTAL	**22**	**69**	**11**	**16**	**55**	**18**

BEARDSTOWN

Player	FG	FGA	FT	FTA	Pts	PF
Art Dufelmeier	3	26	0	2	6	3
Don Ed	0	6	1	1	1	2
Don Goff	0	4	0	1	0	1
Elmer Huss	0	2	0	1	0	4
Jerry Mahnken	0	1	0	0	0	1
Jimmie O'Hara	0	1	1	2	1	0
Harold Osmer	0	0	0	0	0	1

Player	FG	FGA	FT	FTA	Pts	PF
Norm Steele	4	15	0	2	8	2
Dick Stephenson	5	13	3	10	13	2
Fred Wright	0	1	0	0	0	0
TOTAL	12	69	5	19	29	16

Salem	14	10	(24)	15	16	(31) – 55
Beardstown	9	10	(19)	5	5	(10) – 29

189

Herrin (H.S.) 30, Chicago Heights (Bloom Twp.) 25

First Round Game at Champaign [UI, Huff Gym]
Thursday, March 14, 1940

HERRIN (H.S.)

Player	FG	FGA	FT	FTA	Pts	PF
Fred Campbell	4	11	3	3	11	4
Leon Davis	0	4	0	1	0	1
Leonard Hopkins	3	5	0	1	6	1
Dallas Lillich	2	12	5	5	9	2
Junior Newlin	1	4	0	0	2	3
Edward Parsons	1	1	0	1	2	1
TOTAL	**11**	**37**	**8**	**11**	**30**	**12**

CHICAGO HEIGHTS (BLOOM TWP.)

Player	FG	FGA	FT	FTA	Pts	PF
Charles Grupp	1	7	1	3	3	3
Hendron	1	5	3	4	5	0
Nelson	1	3	0	1	2	3
Pieperbrink	0	4	0	0	0	0
Robinson	5	13	1	4	11	3
Scott	2	8	0	2	4	1
TOTAL	**10**	**40**	**5**	**14**	**25**	**10**

Herrin (H.S.)	7	9	(16)	8	6	(14)	– 30
Chicago Heights (Bloom Twp.)	10	5	(15)	7	3	(10)	– 25

Paris 36, Taylorville 35 (OT)

First Round Game at Champaign [UI, Huff Gym]
Thursday, March 14, 1940

PARIS

Player	FG	FGA	FT	FTA	Pts	PF
Ray Chew	3	12	1	1	7	3
Lawrence Humerickhous	0	3	2	2	2	4
Max Pederson	0	3	0	0	0	1
Dale Schiele	7	16	0	2	14	2
Verne Swinford	1	4	0	0	2	4
Walter Switzer	0	0	0	0	0	0
Floyd Wilson	4	10	2	7	10	3
James Wilson	0	4	1	1	1	3
TOTAL	**15**	**52**	**6**	**13**	**36**	**20**

TAYLORVILLE

Player	FG	FGA	FT	FTA	Pts	PF
Gordon Brown	2	8	3	6	7	0
Don Hubbartt	1	10	3	3	5	4
Johnny Jones	0	0	1	2	1	1
Eugene McConkey	0	1	0	2	0	2
Willis Powell	4	6	2	7	10	2
Joe Savaris	1	5	2	3	4	3
Benny Wilhelm	3	15	2	4	8	1
TOTAL	**11**	**45**	**13**	**27**	**35**	**13**

Paris	12	14	(26)	2	6	(8)	2	– 36
Taylorville	8	3	(11)	13	10	(23)	1	– 35

Moline (H.S.) 28, Casey 23

First Round Game at Champaign [UI, Huff Gym]
Thursday, March 14, 1940

MOLINE (H.S.)

Player	FG	FGA	FT	FTA	Pts	PF
Dave Brasmer	2	11	0	1	4	0
Ed Gustafson	2	10	2	4	6	2
Bob Johnson	0	6	0	0	0	1
Bob Miller	2	3	1	3	5	1
Henning Olson	1	5	1	1	3	0
Dick Petrilli	0	0	0	0	0	0
Jack Turner	3	13	4	6	10	3
TOTAL	**10**	**48**	**8**	**15**	**28**	**7**

CASEY

Player	FG	FGA	FT	FTA	Pts	PF
Bill Bertram	1	9	0	0	2	3
Lamont Dehl	0	0	0	0	0	0
Gene Hartman	1	4	1	1	3	4
Marion Kilborn	3	8	1	1	7	0
Denver Mumford	1	11	3	6	5	2
Russell Mumford	0	0	0	0	0	1
Merle Snider	3	12	0	1	6	3
TOTAL	**9**	**44**	**5**	**9**	**23**	**13**

Moline (H.S.)	9	0	(9)	8	11	(19)	– 28
Casey	9	7	(16)	3	4	(7)	– 23

Lewistown 31, Hebron 30

First Round Game at Champaign [UI, Huff Gym]
Thursday, March 14, 1940

LEWISTOWN

Player	FG	FGA	FT	FTA	Pts	PF
Tony Butkovich	5	14	4	4	14	0
Bill Fithian	0	1	0	0	0	1
Donnie Ford	1	2	0	0	2	1
Alan Jackson	1	8	0	0	2	3
Jim Jackson	4	8	1	3	9	0
Mike Nayden	0	4	0	0	0	2
Robert Watson	0	1	0	0	0	0
Harry Wilcoxen	2	8	0	0	4	4
TOTAL	**13**	**6**	**5**	**7**	**31**	**11**

HEBRON

Player	FG	FGA	FT	FTA	Pts	PF
Gordon Burgett	4	17	3	4	11	2
Keith Johnson	4	17	1	2	9	2
Howard Judson	3	7	1	2	7	1
John Kjellstrom	1	13	1	4	3	0
John Ryan	0	2	0	0	0	0
Russell Voltz	0	1	0	0	0	0
TOTAL	**12**	**57**	**6**	**12**	**30**	**5**

Lewistown	6	8	(14)	4	13	(17)	– 31
Hebron	6	8	(14)	10	6	(16)	– 30

Dundee 72, Rushville 47

First Round Game at Champaign [UI, Huff Gym]
Thursday, March 14, 1940

DUNDEE

Player	FG	FGA	FT	FTA	Pts	PF
Robert Ehlert	1	2	1	1	3	0
Richard Heidinger	2	2	0	0	4	4
Clarence Massier	8	20	5	5	21	3
Ken Menke	9	16	2	3	20	3
Richard Menke	6	13	0	0	12	1
Bethard Schuldt	0	2	0	0	0	1
Gerald Schuldt	1	2	0	0	2	0
John Schumacher	3	18	2	2	8	3
Ronald Schumacher	1	8	0	0	2	0
Donald Swanson	0	1	0	0	0	0
TOTAL	**31**	**84**	**10**	**11**	**72**	**15**

RUSHVILLE

Player	FG	FGA	FT	FTA	Pts	PF
Paul Bigham	2	9	7	10	11	1
Dodd Bryant	0	4	3	3	3	2
Cecil Burrows	0	1	0	0	0	0
Donnie Davis	2	7	2	6	6	3
Leo DeCounter	0	0	0	0	0	0
Ed Miles	7	15	2	3	16	1
Clifford Roudebush	0	0	0	0	0	0
Gene Runkle	0	0	0	0	0	0
George Runkle	5	26	1	2	11	1
Don Street	0	0	0	0	0	0
TOTAL	**16**	**62**	**15**	**24**	**47**	**8**

Dundee	12	27	(39)	18	15	(33)	– 72
Rushville	5	16	(21)	16	10	(26)	– 47

Granite City 45, Streator (Twp.) 31

First Round Game at Champaign [UI, Huff Gym]
Thursday, March 14, 1940

GRANITE CITY

Player	FG	FGA	FT	FTA	Pts	PF
Everett Daniels	0	0	0	0	0	0
Dan Eftimoff	1	8	0	0	2	0
George Gages	4	16	2	3	10	2
Andy Hagopian	3	8	1	3	7	1
Edward Hoff	0	0	0	0	0	0
Edward "Ebbie" Muelle	0	1	0	1	0	0
Evon Parsaghian	5	27	2	3	12	1
Andy Phillip	4	13	6	7	14	2
John Markarian	0	0	0	0	0	0
TOTAL	**17**	**73**	**11**	**17**	**45**	**6**

STREATOR (TWP.)

Player	FG	FGA	FT	FTA	Pts	PF
Noble Arnold	2	7	1	2	5	3
Jack Danhoff	4	15	0	0	8	4
Don Davis	4	17	1	1	9	3
Harold "Jack" Donelso	0	3	0	0	0	2
Louis Elko	0	11	1	2	1	0
Don Morris	3	26	0	1	6	2
Patrick Ryan	1	1	0	0	2	0
TOTAL	**14**	**80**	**3**	**6**	**31**	**14**

Granite City	13	13	(26)	9	10	(19)	– 45
Streator (Twp.)	6	17	(23)	8	0	(8)	– 31

Champaign (H.S.) 34, Salem 30

Quarterfinal Game at Champaign [UI, Huff Gym]
Friday, March 15, 1940

CHAMPAIGN (H.S.)

Player	FG	FGA	FT	FTA	Pts	PF
Maurice Dolan	1	2	0	1	2	2
Ray Grierson	2	6	0	0	4	4
Noel Hannah	0	2	0	1	0	0
Sidney McAllister	3	12	1	1	7	1
Don McVey	5	9	1	3	11	3
Jack Moore	0	1	0	0	0	2
John Tarrant	5	18	0	1	10	2
Bill Tull	0	2	0	1	0	1
TOTAL	**16**	**52**	**2**	**8**	**34**	**15**

SALEM

Player	FG	FGA	FT	FTA	Pts	PF
Gerald Brubaker	3	9	1	1	7	2
Bill Finks	0	3	0	2	0	0
Dick Gray	5	15	3	7	13	3
Max McGraw	0	1	0	0	0	0
James Meador	0	1	1	1	1	1
Elton Meredith	3	8	0	1	6	1
Daryl Robb	1	6	1	5	3	2
TOTAL	**12**	**43**	**6**	**17**	**30**	**9**

Champaign (H.S.)	10	12	(22)	5	7	(12) – 34
Salem	2	8	(10)	9	11	(20) – 30

Herrin (H.S.) 29, Paris 22

Quarterfinal Game at Champaign [UI, Huff Gym]
Friday, March 15, 1940

HERRIN (H.S.)

Player	FG	FGA	FT	FTA	Pts	PF
Fred Campbell	4	22	5	5	13	2
Leon Davis	0	4	0	0	0	3
Leonard Hopkins	0	2	0	1	0	1
Dallas Lillich	5	9	4	10	14	3
Junior Newlin	0	2	1	1	1	2
Edward Parsons	0	1	1	3	1	3
TOTAL	**9**	**10**	**11**	**20**	**29**	**14**

PARIS

Player	FG	FGA	FT	FTA	Pts	PF
Ray Chew	0	4	1	1	1	1
Lawrence Humerickhous	1	6	4	5	6	2
Max Pederson	0	0	1	1	1	4
Dale Schiele	2	15	1	1	5	1
Verne Swinford	0	0	0	1	0	4
Norman Throneberg	1	6	2	2	4	1
Floyd Wilson	1	10	3	3	5	2
James Wilson	0	4	0	0	0	1
TOTAL	**4**	**45**	**12**	**14**	**22**	**16**

Herrin (H.S.)	7	11	(15)	8	6	(14)	– 29
Paris	6	6	(12)	5	5	(10)	– 22

Moline (H.S.) 49, Lewistown 32

Quarterfinal Game at Champaign [UI, Huff Gym]
Friday, March 15, 1940

MOLINE (H.S.)

Player	FG	FGA	FT	FTA	Pts	PF
Dave Brasmer	3	10	2	5	8	3
Ed Gustafson	2	5	5	5	9	2
Bob Johnson	6	15	0	1	12	4
William Liljegren	0	0	0	0	0	0
Bob Miller	4	6	1	3	9	3
Henning Olson	1	3	1	1	3	3
Dick Petrilli	3	5	0	0	6	0
Lawrence Sandberg	0	0	0	0	0	0
Jack Turner	1	4	0	0	2	0
TOTAL	**20**	**48**	**9**	**15**	**49**	**15**

LEWISTOWN

Player	FG	FGA	FT	FTA	Pts	PF
Tony Butkovich	2	12	0	1	4	4
Bill Fithian	0	2	0	0	0	0
Donnie Ford	1	5	1	1	3	0
Robert Gallinger	0	0	0	1	0	0
Alan Jackson	1	7	2	6	4	4
Jim Jackson	0	10	1	2	1	3
Mike Nayden	4	10	2	4	10	1
Joe Radosevich	0	1	0	0	0	0
Robert Watson	1	1	0	0	2	0
Harry Wilcoxen	3	10	2	6	8	3
TOTAL	**12**	**58**	**8**	**21**	**32**	**15**

Moline (H.S.)	12	11	(23)	15	11	(26)	– 49
Lewistown	12	6	(18)	11	3	(14)	– 32

Granite City 35, Dundee 30

Quarterfinal Game at Champaign [UI, Huff Gym]
Friday, March 15, 1940

GRANITE CITY

Player	FG	FGA	FT	FTA	Pts	PF
Dan Eftimoff	2	9	0	0	4	0
George Gages	2	11	2	2	6	1
Andy Hagopian	4	7	2	2	10	2
Edward "Ebbie" Muelle	0	1	0	0	0	1
Evon Parsaghian	3	16	1	2	7	1
Andy Phillip	2	15	4	7	8	1
TOTAL	**13**	**59**	**9**	**13**	**35**	**5**

DUNDEE

Player	FG	FGA	FT	FTA	Pts	PF
Richard Heidinger	1	1	0	0	2	2
Clarence Massier	1	7	3	4	5	4
Ken Menke	6	15	1	1	13	3
Richard Menke	0	80	0	0	0	1
Bethard Schuldt	0	3	0	1	0	0
John Schumacher	5	20	0	1	10	2
TOTAL	**13**	**54**	**4**	**7**	**30**	**12**

Granite City	10	6	(16)	10	9	(19)	– 35
Dundee	9	7	(16)	12	2	(14)	– 30

Herrin (H.S.) 21, Champaign (H.S.) 17

Semifinal Game at Champaign [UI, Huff Gym]
Saturday, March 16, 1940

HERRIN (H.S.)

Player	FG	FGA	FT	FTA	Pts	PF
Fred Campbell	2	12	0	1	4	1
Leon Davis	0	2	0	2	0	1
Leonard Hopkins	0	2	0	0	0	0
Dallas Lillich	4	16	6	8	14	1
Junior Newlin	1	3	0	0	2	3
Edward Parsons	0	1	1	1	1	0
TOTAL	**7**	**36**	**7**	**12**	**21**	**6**

CHAMPAIGN (H.S.)

Player	FG	FGA	FT	FTA	Pts	PF
Amos Dickey	0	1	0	0	0	0
Maurice Dolan	0	5	0	0	0	0
Ray Grierson	3	12	1	3	7	3
Noel Hannah	0	1	1	3	1	1
Sidney McAllister	2	8	2	2	6	4
Don McVey	1	9	1	1	3	1
Jack Moore	0	1	0	0	0	1
John Tarrant	0	14	0	0	0	4
Bill Tull	0	0	0	0	0	0
Dean Woody	0	1	0	0	0	1
TOTAL	**6**	**52**	**5**	**9**	**17**	**15**

Herrin (H.S.)	5	4	(9)	8	4	(12)	– 21
Champaign (H.S.)	8	1	(9)	6	2	(8)	– 17

Granite City 41, Moline (H.S.) 38
Semifinal Game at Champaign [UI, Huff Gym]
Saturday, March 16, 1940

GRANITE CITY

Player	FG	FGA	FT	FTA	Pts	PF
Dan Eftimoff	0	7	0	0	0	4
George Gages	5	16	0	0	10	3
Andy Hagopian	6	14	1	4	13	2
Edward Hoff	0	0	0	0	0	0
Edward "Ebbie" Muelle	0	0	0	0	0	0
Evon Parsaghian	0	5	2	2	2	3
Andy Phillip	7	29	2	3	16	2
TOTAL	**18**	**71**	**5**	**9**	**41**	**14**

MOLINE (H.S.)

Player	FG	FGA	FT	FTA	Pts	PF
Dave Brasmer	5	13	0	2	10	1
Ed Gustafson	1	11	0	1	2	1
Bob Johnson	3	9	2	3	8	2
Bob Miller	1	4	1	2	3	1
Henning Olson	3	10	2	3	8	1
Jack Turner	2	11	3	3	7	1
TOTAL	**15**	**58**	**8**	**14**	**38**	**7**

Granite City	13	8	(21)	5	15	(20)	– 41
Moline (H.S.)	14	11	(25)	4	9	(13)	– 38

Moline (H.S.) 51, Champaign (H.S.) 33

Third Place Game at Champaign [UI, Huff Gym]
Saturday, March 16, 1940

MOLINE (H.S.)

Player	FG	FGA	FT	FTA	Pts	PF
Dave Brasmer	5	9	1	8	11	2
Ed Gustafson	2	10	0	2	4	4
Bob Johnson	6	21	4	7	16	2
Howard Johnson	0	2	0	0	0	0
William Liljegren	0	0	1	1	1	0
Bob Miller	1	1	0	0	2	0
Henning Olson	3	6	4	6	10	2
Dick Petrilli	0	0	0	0	0	0
Lawrence Sandberg	0	0	0	0	0	1
Jack Turner	3	16	1	2	7	0
TOTAL	**20**	**65**	**11**	**26**	**51**	**11**

CHAMPAIGN (H.S.)

Player	FG	FGA	FT	FTA	Pts	PF
Amos Dickey	2	6	0	1	4	1
Maurice Dolan	1	5	0	0	2	1
Ray Grierson	1	10	2	4	4	3
Noel Hannah	0	0	0	0	0	0
Sidney McAllister	4	18	1	1	9	2
Don McVey	1	2	4	4	6	1
Jack Moore	1	4	0	0	2	2
John Tarrant	0	10	0	1	0	3
Bill Tull	0	2	0	0	0	0
Dean Woody	3	6	0	2	6	3
TOTAL	**13**	**63**	**7**	**13**	**33**	**16**

Moline (H.S.)	9	13	(22)	14	15	(29)	– 51
Champaign (H.S.)	12	4	(16)	9	8	(17)	– 33

Granite City 24, Herrin (H.S.) 22

Final Game at Champaign [UI, Huff Gym]
Saturday, March 16, 1940

GRANITE CITY

Player	FG	FGA	FT	FTA	Pts	PF
Everett Daniels	0	0	0	0	0	0
Dan Eftimoff	0	8	0	1	0	3
George Gages	2	13	0	1	4	0
Andy Hagopian	0	2	0	1	0	0
Edward Hoff	0	0	0	0	0	0
Edward "Ebbie" Mueller	0	1	0	1	0	0
Evon Parsaghian	2	9	1	2	5	2
Andy Phillip	6	23	3	4	15	3
TOTAL	**10**	**56**	**4**	**10**	**24**	**8**

HERRIN (H.S.)

Player	FG	FGA	FT	FTA	Pts	PF
Fred Campbell	6	20	1	2	13	1
Leon Davis	0	3	0	1	0	2
Dallas Lillich	3	14	1	2	7	2
Junior Newlin	0	2	0	1	0	1
Edward Parsons	1	2	0	2	2	3
TOTAL	**10**	**41**	**2**	**8**	**22**	**9**

Granite City	5	6	(11)	4	9	(13)	− 24
Herrin (H.S.)	10	6	(16)	0	6	(6)	− 22

COMPOSITE TEAM TOTALS

School	G	FG	FGA	FT	FTA	Pts	PF
Moline (H.S.)	4	65	219	36	70	166	40
Granite City	4	58	259	29	49	145	33
Champaign (H.S.)	4	54	223	20	47	128	63
Herrin (H.S.)	4	37	154	28	51	102	41
Dundee	2	44	138	14	18	102	27
Salem	2	34	112	17	33	85	27
Lewistown	2	25	104	13	28	63	26
Paris	2	20	97	18	27	58	36
Rushville	1	16	62	15	24	47	8
Taylorville	1	11	45	13	27	35	13
Streator (Twp.)	1	14	80	3	6	31	14
Hebron	1	12	57	6	12	30	5
Beardstown	1	12	69	5	19	29	16
Chicago (Crane)	1	9	54	7	17	25	14
Chicago Heights (Bloom Twp.)	1	10	40	5	14	25	10
Casey	1	9	44	5	9	23	13

BEARDSTOWN

Player	G	FG	FGA	FT	FTA	Pts	PF
Dick Stephenson	1	5	13	3	10	13	2
Norm Steele	1	4	15	0	2	8	2
Art Dufelmeier	1	3	26	0	2	6	3
Don Ed	1	0	6	1	1	1	2
Jimmie O'Hara	1	0	1	1	2	1	0
Don Goff	1	0	4	0	1	0	1
Elmer Huss	1	0	2	0	1	0	4
Jerry Mahnken	1	0	1	0	0	0	1
Harold Osmer	1	0	0	0	0	0	1
Fred Wright	1	0	1	0	0	0	0

CASEY

Player	G	FG	FGA	FT	FTA	Pts	PF
Marion Kilborn	1	3	8	1	1	7	0
Merle Snider	1	3	12	0	1	6	3
Denver Mumford	1	1	11	3	6	5	2
Gene Hartman	1	1	4	1	1	3	4
Bill Bertram	1	1	9	0	0	2	3
Lamont Dehl	1	0	0	0	0	0	0
Russell Mumford	1	0	0	0	0	0	1

CHAMPAIGN (H.S.)

Player	G	FG	FGA	FT	FTA	Pts	PF
Sidney McAllister	4	13	47	4	5	30	9
John Tarrant	4	13	56	0	3	26	10
Ray Grierson	4	9	40	4	10	22	14
Don McVey	4	7	24	8	13	22	8
Maurice Dolan	4	4	17	1	4	9	4
Dean Woody	3	4	11	1	4	9	5
Amos Dickey	3	2	7	0	1	4	1
Noel Hannah	4	0	4	2	5	2	1
Jack Moore	4	1	10	0	1	2	8
Bill Tull	4	1	7	0	1	2	3

CHICAGO (CRANE)

Player	G	FG	FGA	FT	FTA	Pts	PF
Bernie Goldberg	1	5	21	5	7	15	3
Ed Zuber	1	3	18	1	3	7	1
Ben Erkes	1	1	5	0	2	2	1
Roman Wieszczyk	1	0	4	1	4	1	3
Bernard "Buddy" Burrows	1	0	4	0	0	0	4
Walter Dobranski	1	0	0	0	0	0	0
William Matters	1	0	0	0	0	0	0
Bernard Shapiro	1	0	1	0	1	0	0
Frank Stoikovich	1	0	1	0	0	0	2
Abraham Troop	1	0	0	0	0	0	0

CHICAGO HEIGHTS (BLOOM TWP.)

Player	G	FG	FGA	FT	FTA	Pts	PF
Robinson	1	5	13	1	4	11	3
Hendron	1	1	5	3	4	5	0
Scott	1	2	8	0	2	4	1
Charles Grupp	1	1	7	1	3	3	3
Nelson	1	1	3	0	1	2	3
Pieperbrink	1	0	4	0	0	0	0

DUNDEE

Player	G	FG	FGA	FT	FTA	Pts	PF
Ken Menke	2	15	31	3	4	33	6
Clarence Massier	2	9	27	8	9	26	7
John Schumacher	2	8	38	2	3	18	5
Richard Menke	2	6	21	0	0	12	2
Richard Heidinger	2	3	3	0	0	6	6
Robert Ehlert	1	1	2	1	1	3	0
Gerald Schuldt	1	1	2	0	0	2	0
Ronald Schumacher	1	1	8	0	0	2	0
Bethard Schuldt	2	0	5	0	1	0	1
Donald Swanson	1	0	1	0	0	0	0

GRANITE CITY

Player	G	FG	FGA	FT	FTA	Pts	PF
Andy Phillip	4	19	80	15	21	53	8
George Gages	4	13	56	4	6	30	6
Andy Hagopian	4	13	31	4	10	30	5
Evon Parsaghian	4	10	57	6	9	26	7
Dan Eftimoff	4	3	32	0	1	6	7
Everett Daniels	2	0	0	0	0	0	0
Edward Hoff	3	0	0	0	0	0	0
Edward "Ebbie" Mueller	4	0	3	0	2	0	1
John Markarian	1	0	0	0	0	0	0

HEBRON

Player	G	FG	FGA	FT	FTA	Pts	PF
Gordon Burgett	1	4	17	3	4	11	2
Keith Johnson	1	4	17	1	2	9	2
Howard Judson	1	3	7	1	2	7	1
John Kjellstrom	1	1	13	1	4	3	0
John Ryan	1	0	2	0	0	0	0
Russell Voltz	1	0	1	0	0	0	0

HERRIN (H.S.)

Player	G	FG	FGA	FT	FTA	Pts	PF
Dallas Lillich	4	14	51	16	25	44	8
Fred Campbell	4	16	65	9	11	41	8
Leonard Hopkins	3	3	9	0	2	6	2
Edward Parsons	4	2	5	2	7	6	7
Junior Newlin	4	2	11	1	2	5	9
Leon Davis	4	0	13	0	4	0	7

LEWISTOWN

Player	G	FG	FGA	FT	FTA	Pts	PF
Tony Butkovich	2	7	26	4	5	18	4
Harry Wilcoxen	2	5	18	2	6	12	7
Jim Jackson	2	4	18	2	5	10	3
Mike Nayden	2	4	14	2	4	10	3
Alan Jackson	2	2	15	2	6	6	7
Donnie Ford	2	2	7	1	1	5	1
Robert Watson	2	1	2	0	0	2	0
Bill Fithian	2	0	3	0	0	0	1
Robert Gallinger	1	0	0	0	1	0	0
Joe Radosevich	1	0	1	0	0	0	0

MOLINE (H.S.)

Player	G	FG	FGA	FT	FTA	Pts	PF
Bob Johnson	4	15	51	6	11	36	9
Dave Brasmer	4	15	43	3	16	33	6
Jack Turner	4	9	44	8	11	26	4
Henning Olson	4	8	24	8	11	24	6
Ed Gustafson	4	7	36	7	12	21	9
Bob Miller	4	8	14	3	8	19	5
Dick Petrilli	3	3	5	0	0	6	0
William Liljegren	2	0	0	1	1	1	0
Howard Johnson	1	0	2	0	0	0	0
Lawrence Sandberg	2	0	0	0	0	0	1

PARIS

Player	G	FG	FGA	FT	FTA	Pts	PF
Dale Schiele	2	9	31	1	3	19	3
Floyd Wilson	2	5	20	5	10	15	5
Ray Chew	2	3	16	2	2	8	4
Lawrence Humerickhouse	2	1	9	6	7	8	6
Norman Throneberg	1	1	6	2	2	4	1
Verne Swinford	2	1	4	0	1	2	8
Max Pederson	2	0	3	1	1	1	5
James Wilson	2	0	8	1	1	1	4
Walter Switzer	1	0	0	0	0	0	0

RUSHVILLE

Player	G	FG	FGA	FT	FTA	Pts	PF
Ed Miles	1	7	15	2	3	16	1
Paul Bigham	1	2	9	7	10	11	1
George Runkle	1	5	26	1	2	11	1
Donnie Davis	1	2	7	2	6	6	3
Dodd Bryant	1	0	4	3	3	3	2
Cecil Burrows	1	0	1	0	0	0	0
Leo DeCounter	1	0	0	0	0	0	0
Clifford Roudebush	1	0	0	0	0	0	0
Gene Runkle	1	0	0	0	0	0	0
Don Street	1	0	0	0	0	0	0

SALEM

Player	G	FG	FGA	FT	FTA	Pts	PF
Dick Gray	2	9	29	5	10	23	7
Elton Meredith	2	10	30	3	4	23	3
Gerald Brubaker	2	7	14	3	4	17	5
Daryl Robb	2	3	15	3	7	9	5
Bill Finks	2	3	15	1	3	7	4
James Meador	2	2	4	2	4	6	3
Henry Hinckley	1	0	1	0	1	0	0
Max McGraw	2	0	3	0	0	0	0
Bob Scoles	1	0	0	0	0	0	0
Jim Somer	1	0	1	0	0	0	0

STREATOR (TWP.)

Player	G	FG	FGA	FT	FTA	Pts	PF
Don Davis	1	4	17	1	1	9	3
Jack Danhoff	1	4	15	0	0	8	4
Don Morris	1	3	26	0	1	6	2
Noble Arnold	1	2	7	1	2	5	3
Patrick Ryan	1	1	1	0	0	2	0
Louis Elko	1	0	11	1	2	1	0
Harold "Jack" Donelson	1	0	3	0	0	0	2

TAYLORVILLE

Player	G	FG	FGA	FT	FTA	Pts	PF
Willis Powell	1	4	6	2	7	10	2
Benny Wilhelm	1	3	15	2	4	8	1
Gordon Brown	1	2	8	3	6	7	0
Don Hubbartt	1	1	10	3	3	5	4
Joe Savaris	1	1	5	2	3	4	3
Johnny Jones	1	0	0	1	2	1	1
Eugene McConkey	1	0	1	0	2	0	2

Andy Phillip's Career NBA Statistics

Season	Team	G	FGM	FGA	PCT	REB
1947-48	Chicago Stags	32	143	425	.336	—
1948-49	Chicago Stags	60	285	818	.348	—
1949-50	Chicago Stags	65	284	814	.349	—
1950-51	Philadelphia Warriors	66	275	690	.399	446
1951-52	Philadelphia Warriors	66	279	762	.366	434
1952-53	Philadelphia-Ft. Wayne	70	250	629	.397	364
1953-54	Ft. Wayne Pistons	71	255	680	.375	265
1954-55	Ft. Wayne Pistons	64	202	545	.371	290
1955-56	Ft. Wayne Pistons	70	148	405	.365	257
1956-57	Boston Celtics	67	105	277	.379	181
1957-58	Boston Celtics	70	97	273	.355	158
Career Totals		**701**	**2,323**	**6,318**	**.368**	**2,395**
Playoff Totals		**67**	**137**	**137**	**.327**	**205**

Andy Phillip's Career NBA Statistics

Season	AST	PTS	RPG	APG	PPG
1947-48	74	349	—	2.3	10.8
1948-49	319	718	—	5.3	12.0
1949-50	377	758	—	5.8	11.7
1950-51	414	740	6.8	6.3	11.2
1951-52	539	790	6.6	8.2	12.0
1952-53	397	722	5.2	5.7	10.3
1953-54	449	751	3.7	6.3	10.6
1954-55	491	617	4.5	7.7	9.6
1955-56	410	408	3.7	5.9	5.8
1956-57	168	298	2.7	2.5	4.4
1957-58	121	236	2.3	1.7	3.4
Career Totals	**3,759**	**6,384**	**4.4**	**5.4**	**9.1**
Playoff Totals	**293**	**428**	**3.3**	**3.7**	**6.4**

Note: Rebounds were not recorded as an official statistic until the 1950-51 season.

ACKNOWLEDGEMENTS

Quite simply, this book would not be what it is, were it not for the abundant helping hand of Babe Champion, a man who lives up to his impressive name. Granite City should consider itself extremely fortunate to have a man like him in its midst. Quite simply, Babe (Granite City, Class of '51) gets things done. He, and his partner Gus Lignoul (Granite City, Class of '46), were instrumental in supplying me with old newspaper articles about the Happy Warriors from the Press-Record, as well as phone numbers of survivors of past team members.

Writing about an event that happened 67 years earlier, with just a handful of survivors remaining, is difficult enough to pull off. Without someone like Babe pointing me in the right direction, it would have been next to impossible.

Andy Hagopian and John Markarian, the last two survivors of the squad, were a pure joy to deal with and provided the core material for this book. To me, they represent what the Happy Warriors were all about...intelligent, strong, decent, hard-working men, who gave all they had for their community.

And, I promise I'll get Andy's scrapbook back to him one of these days.

Also, thanks go to contributors, Harold Brown, who had some wonderful stories to tell and some great insight to share, Helen Gages, Corky Phillip, Robert Phillip, Queenie Elieff, Isabel Vartan, Joe Astroth, Kenny Parker, Dick King and Patrick Heston.

– Dan Manoyan

ABOUT THE AUTHOR

Dan Manoyan is a sports writer at the Milwaukee Journal Sentinel, where he has worked for the past 15 years. He has won numerous awards for his writing, both at a state and national level. A native of Waukegan, Ill. and graduate of the University of Illinois, Manoyan previously worked as a sports writer at the Kenosha (Wis.) News, the Waukegan (Ill.) News-Sun, and the Dallas Morning News. He has two sons, Eddie and Randy.